THE TEEN ENTREPRENEUR

Anthony Masala

An Integrated Computer Applications and Entrepreneurship Simulation

B.E. Publishing

ISBN 978-0-972133-18-0

Published by
B.E. Publishing
P. O. Box 8558 • Warwick, RI 02888
U.S.A.

For more information, visit www.bepublishing.com

Copyright

B.E. Publishing

The Teen Entrepreneur
Published by B.E. Publishing

Author
Anthony Masala

Editors
Michael Gecawich
Kathleen Hicks
Monica Handy
Diane Silvia
Linda Viveiros
Joy Tavano
Lisa Wardle

Student Reviewers
Joe Brogno
Karen Catoia

Preface

Welcome to *The Teen Entrepreneur*:
An Integrated Computer Applications and Entrepreneurship Simulation

This simulation has been developed to provide teenage-level students with an in-depth, real-world experience in creating a comprehensive business plan for a student-selected teen-based business.

The Teen Entrepreneur contains a collection of 21 individual projects designed to give students hands-on practice in using their computer skills to create a variety of standard business plan documents and marketing materials for their own business.

The simulation uses a self-guided, personalized teaching and learning style. The goal of the simulation is to have students create a business plan and supporting marketing materials that they can use to start their own real business while still attending school.

The book is modeled after the National Business Education Association's National Standard for Business Education for Entrepreneurship. Students who complete this simulation will learn how to recognize a business opportunity, start a business based on the recognized opportunity, and then develop a comprehensive business plan to learn how to operate and maintain the business.

To create their business plan and marketing materials for their business, students will use a variety of Microsoft Office software applications to create accounting, financial, marketing, and management documents.

About the Author

Anthony Masala is currently an office technology instructor at the Career Tech Center of the Herkimer County Board of Cooperative Educational Services in Herkimer, New York, a vocational and technical institute servicing students in grades 11 and 12, as well as adult learners.

In addition to his full-time duties as office instructional instructor, Mr. Masala is employed as a virtual university instructor for the Utica School of Commerce, a private business and technology college. He served for a period of nine years as a member of his local board of education, three of which he served as president. Prior to entering the field of education, Mr. Masala was employed for a period of 22 years in various management capacities in both for-profit and non-profit organizations. During this time, he also owned and managed his own business.

Mr. Masala is an advocate for business education and continues to inspire entrepreneurial spirit in his students.

Table of Contents

Table of Contents Continued

Stay Inspired: Real Teen Entrepreneur Success Stories

Section 1:
Introduction

1.1   Welcome to The Teen Entrepreneur

The Teen Entrepreneur simulation has been developed to provide teenage-level entrepreneur and business students with in-depth, real-world experience in starting a real teen-based business.

By completing a series of integrated hands-on projects that combine the concepts of entrepreneurship and computer skills, *The Teen Entrepreneur* will guide you through the process of creating a real business plan for a business that you choose to start and operate.

Throughout the simulation, you will be challenged to use creativity, entrepreneurial, writing, and decision-making skills that will yield a professional business plan and marketing materials. The business plan can then be used as a guide to help you operate and manage your chosen business.

Get ready to embark on one of the best educational experiences of your life in *The Teen Entrepreneur*!

1.2   Who Should Use This Book?

This book is designed for teenage students who are enrolled in a secondary level business, entrepreneurship, and/or technology course. This book is ideal for teaching teenage students how to:

1. start and operate a business.
2. create a business plan using computer application software.
3. apply entrepreneurial skills to start a real teen-based business.

1.3   Your Role in This Simulation

In *The Teen Entrepreneur*, you will assume the role of a teen-based business owner. The form of business ownership you will assume will be that of a sole proprietorship. A **sole proprietorship** is a business owned and operated by one person.

As a business owner in this simulation, you will be required to:

1. choose a teen-based business to own and operate.
2. complete a series of individual projects to successfully create a comprehensive business plan for your chosen business.

1.4 Why Start Your Own Teen Business?

One of the greatest privileges afforded by the U.S. economic system is the ability for any U.S. citizen to own and operate his or her own business, known as **Free Enterprise**.

Owning your own business has many rewards and challenges. As previously mentioned, you will be assuming the role of a sole proprietor in this simulation. Let's take a look at some of the advantages and disadvantages to owning your own business as a sole proprietorship:

Advantages to Owning Your Own Business as a Sole Proprietorship:

1. The business is usually easy to start.
2. You are your own boss; consequently, you get to make all of the business decisions.
3. You get to use your knowledge and skills to run and operate the business.
4. You control your income.
5. You develop the ability to take risks.
6. If applicable, you get to introduce new products to the market.
7. You learn the value of self-discipline and time-management skills.
8. You can learn more about how business works.

Disadvantages to Owning Your Own Business as a Sole Proprietorship:

1. You have to be prepared to work long hours, especially in the startup phase.
2. You have to provide the necessary startup money, known as **capital**.
3. You are responsible for money owed, known as **debt**.
4. The business is dependent on your health and ability to continue working.
5. You have to be prepared to find an alternate source of income if the business fails.

1.5 What You Will Learn from This Book

After successfully completing *The Teen Entrepreneur*, you will learn how to:
1. select an appropriate teen-based business to own and operate.
2. create and write a comprehensive business plan for a teen-based business.
3. use and integrate several software application programs to create a professional business plan.
4. organize computer files.
5. apply technical writing skills in developing a business plan.
6. use creativity and design skills to produce the required documents in a business plan.
7. use decision-making skills as they pertain to creating a business plan.
8. apply entrepreneurship concepts to an individualized business.

1.6 Requirements of This Simulation

To complete the individual projects in this simulation, you will need the following:

1. *The Teen Entrepreneur* Data CD-ROM installed on your hard drive or network drive. (See section 3 for more detailed instructions.)

2. The following software applications:
   - Microsoft Word
   - Microsoft Excel
   - Microsoft Publisher (or an equivalent desktop publishing software)
   - Microsoft Access
   - Microsoft FrontPage (or an equivalent Web Page design software)
   - Adobe Acrobat Reader
   - A drawing or illustration program such as Adobe Illustrator, Adobe Photoshop, or Microsoft Paint

3. Three-ring view binder (optional)

1.7 Prerequisite Skills

To complete the projects in this simulation, the student should have a basic working knowledge of the following software applications:

- Microsoft Word
- Microsoft Excel
- Microsoft Publisher (or an equivalent desktop publishing software)
- Microsoft Access
- Microsoft FrontPage (or an equivalent Web Page design software)
- Drawing or illustration software

Note: This simulation does not provide step-by-step instructions on how to use any of the software applications listed above.

1.8 Table of Projects, Completion Time, and Software Required

The individual projects you will complete in this simulation are provided in the table below. This table also includes the approximate completion time and software required to complete each project. This simulation will take approximately 23-28 hours to complete. This table should be used as a guide for planning your classroom schedule to complete this simulation.

	The Teen Entrepreneur Table of Projects, Completion Time, and Software Required		
Project #	**Project Title**	**Approx. Time Required** (in hours)	**Software Required**
1	Choosing Your Teen-based Business	1	Microsoft Word
2	Creating the Company Description	1.5	Microsoft Word
3	Creating a Logo and Tagline	1-2	Drawing or illustration software, Adobe Acrobat Reader
4	Creating the Description of Products and Services	1	Microsoft Word
5	Creating the Market Analysis	1-1.5	Microsoft Word
6	Creating a Business Card	1	Microsoft Word, Publisher (or any desktop publishing software), Adobe Acrobat Reader
7	Creating Company Letterhead	.5	Microsoft Word, Adobe Acrobat Reader
8	Creating the Marketing Plan	1	Microsoft Word
9	Creating the Operating Plan	1	Microsoft Word
10	Creating a Schedule of Startup Funds Required	1	Microsoft Excel
11	Creating a Customer Prospect Database	2	Microsoft Access, Adobe Acrobat Reader
12	Creating an Introductory Promotional Letter	1.5	Microsoft Word and Access
13	Creating a Three-Panel Brochure	2-3	Microsoft Publisher (or any desktop publishing software), Adobe Acrobat Reader
14	Creating a Newspaper Advertisement	1	Microsoft Word, Publisher (or any desktop publishing software), Adobe Acrobat Reader
15	Creating an Owner's Resume	1	Microsoft Word, Adobe Acrobat Reader
16	Creating a Projected Income Statement	1	Microsoft Excel, Adobe Acrobat Reader
17	Creating a Promotional Slide Show	1-2	Microsoft Word, PowerPoint, Adobe Acrobat Reader
18	Creating the Executive Summary	1	Microsoft Word
19	Creating the Business Plan Cover Page	.5	Microsoft Word
20	Final Assembly of Your Business Plan	1	None
*21	Creating a Web Site Homepage (optional)	1-2	Microsoft FrontPage (or any Web site design software)

*Project 21 is an optional part of the simulation. Check with your instructor to see if you are required to complete this project.

Section 2:
Meet Your Teen
Entrepreneur Navigator:
Shaun Decker

ABOUT THIS SECTION:

Throughout this simulation, you will be guided by a teen entrepreneur named Shaun Decker. This section introduces Shaun Decker to the reader. It is recommended that you read this section before beginning this simulation.

INCLUDED IN THIS SECTION:

2.1 Meet Shaun Decker: Your Teen Entrepreneur Navigator

Throughout this simulation, you will be guided every step of the way by a real teen entrepreneur, Shaun Decker, an industrious 18-year-old high school senior who is about to start his own business.

2.2 Background Information About Shaun Decker

Shaun resides in Pleasant Landing, New York, with his parents, Jeff and Caroline Decker. After graduating from high school, Shaun will be attending his local community college where he plans to major in business administration and management. After completing his two years of study at the community college, Shaun plans on transferring to a four-year college to complete the final two years of his bachelor's degree. He is a sports enthusiast, particularly interested in soccer and hockey, which he has played throughout his high school years. He is a drummer in the high school band and a strong baritone in the high school chorus. Shaun is also president of his high school's Future Business Leaders of America chapter and treasurer of his senior class.

2.3 Shaun Decker's Business Scenario

In order to start his business, Shaun Decker needs a $5,000 startup loan, which he is seeking to borrow from his parents.

Before they loan Shaun the money, however, Shaun's parents have requested that Shaun prepare a business plan to present to them. If Shaun's business plan convinces his parents that his new business has the potential to be successful, they have agreed to provide the startup loan to Shaun, allowing him to start his business.

In this simulation, you will learn first-hand how Shaun Decker went about preparing his business plan to obtain a startup loan from his parents. While the business you choose to start for this simulation will probably differ from Shaun Decker's, the format of your own business plan will be similar. In this simulation, Shaun Decker's business plan is designed to serve as a guide for you as you create your own business plan.

SEE IT IN ACTION
with Shaun Decker

Shaun Decker's teen entrepreneurship story unfolds in the "See It In Action with Shaun Decker" section provided within each project.

Section 3:
Using This Book and
the Data CD

ABOUT THIS SECTION:

This section provides important information that will help you understand how to read this book and use *The Teen Entrepreneur* Data CD to complete this simulation. It is recommended that you read this section to become familiar with the format of this book.

INCLUDED IN THIS SECTION:

3.1   Understanding the Format of This Book

This simulation has been organized into an easy-to-read, self-guided, step-by-step format that includes a total of 21 projects. What follows is a brief explanation of the individual sections that make up each project in this simulation. It is recommended that you read this section to become familiar with the format of this book.

3.2   How Each Project is Organized

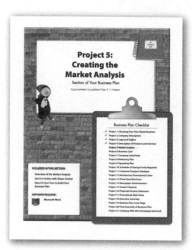

Title Page

Each new project begins with a project title page. The project title page provides the student with the following:

- The project number and title
- The approximate time it takes to complete the project
- The contents of each project
- The software required to complete the project
- A "Business Plan Checklist"

Project Overview

The project overview provides the student with the following:

- The objective of the project
- Important background information about each new project

See It In Action with Shaun Decker

The "See It In Action with Shaun Decker" section provides the student with the following:

- An overview of how Shaun Decker created each component of his business plan
- Actual examples of each component of Shaun Decker's business plan

Now It's Your Turn to Build Your Business Plan

The "Now It's Your Turn to Build Your Business Plan" section provides the student with the following:

- Instructions for the student to follow to complete each project

3.3   Stay Inspired with Real Teen Entrepreneur Stories

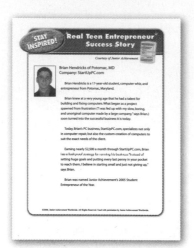

To keep the student inspired, there are real teen entrepreneur success stories included after various projects in this simulation. The teen entrepreneur stories are provided courtesy of *Junior Achievement Worldwide*.

3.4 Using The Teen Entrepreneur Data CD

The Teen Entrepreneur simulation is designed to be used in conjunction with *The Teen Entrepreneur* Data CD. The files on the Data CD are compatible with Microsoft Windows applications. *The Teen Entrepreneur* Data CD must be installed on your computer before you begin this simulation. The Data CD contains a variety of data files, templates, and worksheets that will assist you in completing each project in this simulation.

Install *The Teen Entrepreneur* Data CD prior to beginning this simulation.

3.5 Installing the Data CD

Instructions for installing the Data CD:
1. Place the Data CD in your computer's CD-ROM drive.
2. The CD Install Menu should open automatically. Follow the on-screen instructions.
3. If the Install Menu does not open automatically, open the contents of the CD while in the CD-ROM drive and double-click on the "Install.exe" file. Follow the on-screen instructions.
4. Alternately, you can simply Copy the folder titled "Teen Entrepreneur" located on the CD and Paste it to your hard drive or network drive.

Once installed, the data files can be accessed from a folder titled "Teen Entrepreneur" from your computer's hard drive or network drive.

3.6 Saving Your Project Files

It is important that the project files in this simulation are saved in the same folder on your hard drive or network drive.

Before beginning this simulation, do the following:

Create a new folder on your hard drive or network drive titled "My Business Plan." All completed project files should be saved in this folder.

Section 4:
Entrepreneurs and
Business Plans

Since you will be assuming the role of a teen entrepreneur and creating your own business plan in this book, it is important to understand what an entrepreneur and a business plan are. It is recommended that you read this section before beginning this simulation.

INCLUDED IN THIS SECTION:

4.1   What is an Entrepreneur?

An **entrepreneur** is a person who organizes, operates, and assumes the risk for a business venture. Most commonly, the term entrepreneur applies to someone who establishes a new entity (or business) to offer a new or existing product or service into a new or existing market, whether for a profit or not-for-profit outcome.

Some famous American entrepreneurs include: Henry Ford (Ford Motor Company), Dave Thomas (Wendy's), Thomas Edison (for the invention of electricity and light bulbs), Milton S. Hershey (Hershey Company), Bill Gates (Microsoft), and Steve Jobs (Apple Computers).

To start a new business, all entrepreneurs need a *business plan*, which is discussed in more detail below.

4.2   What is a Business Plan and Why Have One?

A **business plan** is a series of documents that serves as a blueprint for building a business. A business plan includes information about the business, the industry in which it competes, its products and/or services, its customers, its competitors, and its finances. Because starting a business can be an overwhelming task, business plans allow business owners to break the process down into small, easy-to-manage sections.

A business plan indicates:
1. The current status of the business: Is the business in the startup, growth, or decline stage?
2. The vision of the business: What are the future goals and objectives of the business?
3. A plan to achieve the vision of the business

The primary functions of a business plan are:
1. To set goals and objectives for the business to follow.
2. To attract potential investors.
3. To acquire financing.
4. To attract quality employees.
5. To attract potential new customers.

4.3   Components of a Business Plan

It is important to note that most business plans are not identical. In fact, depending on the type of business, business plans can look very different.

Table 4.1 highlights the most common components of a business plan. Each of these components is discussed in more detail in the individual projects within this simulation.

Table 4.1

Typical Components of a Business Plan	
Cover Page	The cover page usually includes the company name and address information, the author of the business plan, and the date the business plan was prepared.
Executive Summary	A section that summarizes all of the sections of the business plan. The Executive Summary is always the first section in a business plan and must immediately capture the attention of the reader and entice him/her to inquire further and read the remainder of the plan.
Company Description	A section that includes details about the business including its age, history, legal form of ownership (sole proprietorship, partnership, or corporation), industry classification (retail, wholesale, manufacturing, services), structure, location, the number of employees, and its primary function(s).
Description of Products and Services	A section that provides detailed information about the products and/or services offered to customers.
Market Analysis	A section that provides detailed information and analysis of the conditions and trends in an industry including the target market of the business, demographics of the target market, and a detailed analysis of the competition.
Marketing Plan	A section that includes plans for maintaining and building the customer base, the benefits to the customer of choosing this business over competitors', pricing information, and promotion and advertising plans.
Operating Plan	A section that details the operations of the business from acquiring materials and supplies to the distribution of the products and/or services to customers.
Funds Required and Expected Uses	A section that is necessary when seeking investors or bank financing and shows detailed plans for the use of any funds and plans for repayment if a loan is necessary.
Financial Statements	A section that includes a Statement of Profit/Loss, a Balance Sheet, a Statement of Cash Flow for the past three years (if an existing business), and three-year projections (existing business and startup business).
Owner's Credentials (Resume)	While not always included, some business plans include a resume of the owner. This provides readers with the professional background and work experience of the owner of the business.
Supplemental Attachments	In addition to the standard components discussed above, some business plans include additional documents and marketing materials to provide the reader with a better vision of the business.

4.4   Characteristics of a Good Business Plan

Although most business plans are not identical, every business plan should be:
- Neat
- Organized
- Professional
- Well-written and well-designed
- Highlight important aspects of the business

4.5   How Long is a Typical Business Plan?

The length of a typical business plan can vary ranging from 10 to 100 pages in length. The length of a business plan depends on the intended use of the plan and its audience.

4.6   Components of the Business Plan You Will Create

Since you will be required to choose a new business to run and operate in this simulation, the business plan you will create will be modeled after a "Startup Business Plan." The components of the business plan you will create are provided below in Table 4.2.

Table 4.2

Components of the Business Plan You Will Create in this Simulation

Cover Page	Supplemental Attachments including:
Executive Summary	Logo and Tagline
Company Description	Business Card
Description of Products and Services	Company Letterhead
Market Analysis	Customer Prospect Database
Marketing Plan	Promotional Letter
Operating Plan	Brochure
Schedule of Startup Funds Required	Advertisement
Projected Income Statement (for Year 1)	Slide Show Presentation
Owner's Resume	Company Web Site Homepage (optional)

Section 5:
The Individual Projects in This Simulation

Project 1: Choosing Your Teen-based Business

Project 2: Creating the Company Description

Project 3: Creating a Logo and Tagline

Project 4: Creating the Description of Products and Services

Project 5: Creating the Market Analysis

Project 6: Creating a Business Card

Project 7: Creating Company Letterhead

Project 8: Creating the Marketing Plan

Project 9: Creating the Operating Plan

Project 10: Creating a Schedule of Startup Funds Required

Project 11: Creating a Customer Prospect Database

Project 12: Creating an Introductory Promotional Letter

Project 13: Creating a Three-Panel Brochure

Project 14: Creating a Newspaper Advertisement

Project 15: Creating an Owner's Resume

Project 16: Creating a Projected Income Statement

Project 17: Creating a Promotional Slide Show

Project 18: Creating the Executive Summary

Project 19: Creating the Business Plan Cover Page

Project 20: Final Assembly of Your Business Plan

Project 21: Creating a Web Site Homepage (*optional*)

Project 1:
Choosing Your
Teen-based Business

Approximate Completion Time: 1 hour

MY BUSINESS PLAN

Business Plan Checklist

INCLUDED IN THIS SECTION:

- Overview of Choosing Your Teen-based Business
- See It In Action with Shaun Decker
- Now It's Your Turn to Build Your Business Plan

SOFTWARE REQUIRED:

- Microsoft Word

Choosing Your Teen-based Business

THE TEEN ENTREPRENEUR

YOUR OBJECTIVE:

• To choose a Teen-based Business to start and operate

BACKGROUND INFORMATION BEFORE YOU BEGIN:

What Business Do I Start?

All aspiring entrepreneurs, whether they be young or old, have one important question to answer: What business do I choose to start? There are many factors to consider when choosing what business you will start and run. This section will provide you with some important factors to consider before you choose your teen-based business.

Major Factors to Consider Before Selecting Your Business

When selecting a business for this simulation, consider the following factors:

1. **What are your interests?**
   When considering your interests, ask yourself these questions:
   - *What do I like to do?*
   - *What are the talents that I possess and enjoy?*
   - *Do I like working with people?*

2. **What are your abilities?**
   When considering your abilities, ask yourself what you are good at. If you like taking pictures, you might consider starting a photography business. If you enjoy cooking or baking, perhaps a food service business would be a good fit for you. The important thing is to choose a business for or which builds upon a skill or talent that you already possess.

3. **Do you have the startup money and necessary resources?**
   Every business, no matter how large or small, requires money (known as capital) and other resources in order to get started. Before choosing a business, you will need to answer these questions:

• *Do I have enough money to start the business? If not, where will I get the money?*
• *Do I possess the resources required to start the business? If not, where will they come from?*

Let's say you are considering starting a house painting business. To start the painting business, you will need paint brushes, ladders, drop cloths, and of course, paint. These items cost money. You need to have these items before you can perform your first painting job. If you cannot afford to buy the required items to start the business, this would not be a good choice for your business.

4. Profit potential

Since businesses operate to make a profit, one of the most important factors to consider is your potential market. In other words, will consumers buy what you are selling? For instance, let's say you decide to start your own surfboard maintenance service company. If you live in an area that is far from the ocean, chances are you will have a difficult time securing new customers for your service.

5. Pleasure

When considering what business you will start, remember that it is important to enjoy what you are doing. After all, if your business takes off, you will be spending a considerable amount of time on the job. Just imagine going to a job you hate every day. Yuk!

6. Availability

Since you are still attending school, you will have to consider when you will be available to operate your business. It doesn't make sense to start a business that you can't invest the necessary time it will take to make it successful.

Explore the Occupational Outlook Handbook Web Site

A great place to explore possible businesses you can start is the Occupational Outlook Handbook Web site at *www.bls.gov/oco/*. Sponsored by the U.S. Bureau of Labor Statistics, the Occupational Outlook Handbook Web site includes information on hundreds of careers. Click on the "A-Z Index" to explore possible businesses to start. While most of the list is dedicated to providing information on career titles for job seekers, you can use the list to brainstorm different business opportunities and possibilities.

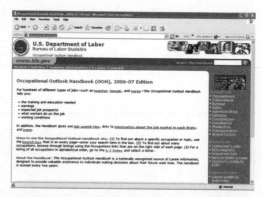

Check out the Occupational Outlook Handbook Web site to explore possible businesses you can start at *www.bls.gov/oco/*

What Are Some Possible Teen-based Businesses You Can Start?

There are literally hundreds of teen-based businesses you can start. However, you need to decide what is right for you. The list of possible teen-based businesses provided in Table 1.1 will help you get started. As you read the list, take note of the types of businesses that most appeal to you.

Table 1.1

Possible Teen-based Businesses to Consider Starting

- Landscaping
- Mobile Car Wash/Car Detailing
- Bicycle Repair
- Child Care
- Pet Grooming
- Pet Care (Sitting/Walking)
- Arts & Crafts
- Pet Treats
- Gutter Cleaning Service
- CD Replication

- Food Preparation/Cooking
- General Cleaning Service
- Desktop Publishing
- PC Tutoring
- Academic Tutoring
- House Painting
- Freelance Writer
- Artist
- Photographer
- Music Instructor
- Hairstyling

Note: Check with your instructor and/or local Chamber of Commerce to see if the type of business you are considering requires a business license and/or insurance to operate.

Now let's learn how Shaun Decker chose his Teen-based Business

How Shaun Decker Chose His Business

How It All Started

Shaun has been interested in business since age nine when he opened a street-side lemonade stand and car wash business. At age 12, he closed the lemonade stand and car wash business and started a lawn maintenance business, which he has operated very profitably since its inception. Over the years, he has managed to bank nearly $15,000 of that profit to help offset the cost of his college education. During the winter months, when lawn maintenance was no longer necessary, Shaun worked part-time at an area retailer. He recently lost that job when the owner retired and closed the business.

Rather than look for another part-time job, Shaun believed he could make more money running a business of his own. From his business courses at school and his past experience with operating a business, Shaun knew that he possessed all of the personal qualities of a successful business entrepreneur. Before choosing a new business to start, Shaun identified and wrote the following qualities about himself:

Qualities I possess:

1. **Excellent work ethic.** I am a hard worker and very self-motivated.

2. **Strong sense of responsibility.** I am very responsible and self-disciplined.

3. **Self-confidence.** I am very confident in my business and technical abilities.

4. **Creativity and innovation.** I am very creative, always looking for new opportunities.

5. **Goal oriented.** I set high goals for myself and develop plans for attaining these goals.

6. **Risk tolerant.** I am not afraid of taking the occasional risk if the probability of a successful outcome is good.

7. **Ability to multi-task.** I can juggle all of my responsibilities including family, classmates, teammates, and work.

As someone who has already recognized and taken advantage of business opportunities by planning, organizing, and managing small businesses of his own, and making a profit in the process, Shaun is already a successful entrepreneur.

Working for someone else has its advantages, like the security of a steady paycheck and a stable work schedule. It also has disadvantages, like a fixed rate of pay and a work schedule that often conflicts with other obligations and weekend activities that may arise. Shaun prefers the personal satisfaction, independence, freedom, and creative challenges that he derives from operating his own business enterprise. Despite uncertain income, the possible loss of any money he originally invests in the business, and the long hours required of owning and operating a business, Shaun believes it is worth the risk.

Shaun Decker's New Business

Shaun decided that the logical choice for his new business would be desktop publishing for the following reasons:

1. Shaun loves to work with computers, and this type of business really interests him.

2. Shaun believes his technical skills and experience with computer applications software would add to the potential for business success. A fast and accurate typist, Shaun has been paid by friends and classmates to transfer their handwritten essays and research papers to the typed page. He has also been paid for designing and developing Web pages for friends of his parents that own small businesses in his community.

3. Shaun believes that the profit potential of this type of business could be very attractive.

4. Thanks to the profits earned from his lawn maintenance business, Shaun already has most of the required equipment to start a desktop publishing business. Shaun owns a state-of-the-art computer system, digital camera, and word processing, spreadsheet, database, presentation, desktop publishing, and Web design software.

Startup Needs for Shaun's Business

Through doing some Internet research on the desktop publishing industry, Shaun decided that, in addition to his own equipment, he would need the following items to start his business:

- Flatbed scanner
- Laser printer
- Notebook computer
- Variety of paper
- Laser printer toner
- Variety of office supplies

Shaun estimated he would need about $5,000 to cover the cost of starting his desktop publishing business.

Why Shaun Decker Needs a Business Plan

Shaun decided to discuss his business idea with his parents, and, while his parents were interested in the idea, they did not like the thought of him depleting his college savings to start the business. They proposed, instead, that he develop a formal business plan and present it to them as potential lenders. If the proposal looked feasible, they would consider loaning the initial $5,000 to him, which he could then repay, interest free, from the eventual profits of the business. Shaun jumped on the opportunity offered by his parents and immediately started researching business plan formats and the information required to develop a professional business plan.

> Throughout the remainder of this simulation, you will learn how Shaun Decker developed his business plan while also creating your own. Remember, the purpose of Shaun's business plan will be to convince his parents to give him a startup loan. Assume that you have a similar scenario in which you will also require a loan to start your new business. Your lender has requested that you present him with a business plan to see if your new business is worthy of granting you the startup loan.
>
> Good luck as you enter the world of teen entrepreneurship!

Now it's your turn to choose your Teen-based Business

Project 1:
Choose Your Teen-based Business

Follow the instructions provided below.

1. Using Microsoft Word, retrieve the file "Project1_Worksheet" from the "Teen Entrepreneur" folder installed from the Data CD.
2. Type your name and the current date in the header section of page 1 in the document.
3. Follow the instructions provided in the document to complete the worksheet.
4. Carefully proofread your work for accuracy and format.
5. If you have not done so already, create a new folder on your hard drive or network drive. Name the folder "My Business Plan." *All future files created throughout this simulation should be saved to this new folder.*
6. Save the completed file as "Project1_Choice" to the "My Business Plan" folder.
7. Print a copy of the document. Discuss the results of the worksheet with your instructor for approval to proceed with this simulation.

At this point, you should now have selected a business to run and operate. The remainder of the projects in this simulation will guide you through the process of creating a business plan for your chosen business.

Project 2: Creating the Company Description

Section of Your Business Plan

Approximate Completion Time: 1.5 hours

Business Plan Checklist

✓ Project 1:   Choosing Your Teen-based Business

Project 2:   Company Description

Project 3:   Logo and Tagline

Project 4:   Description of Products and Services

Project 5:   Market Analysis

Project 6:   Business Card

Project 7:   Company Letterhead

Project 8:   Marketing Plan

Project 9:   Operating Plan

Project 10:   Schedule of Startup Funds Required

Project 11:   Customer Prospect Database

Project 12:   Introductory Promotional Letter

Project 13:   Three-Panel Brochure

Project 14:   Newspaper Advertisement

Project 15:   Owner's Resume

Project 16:   Projected Income Statement

Project 17:   Promotional Slide Show

Project 18:   Executive Summary

Project 19:   Business Plan Cover Page

Project 20:   Final Assembly of Your Business Plan

Project 21:   Company Web Site Homepage (*optional*)

INCLUDED IN THIS SECTION:

- Overview of the Company Description
- See It In Action with Shaun Decker
- Now It's Your Turn to Build Your Business Plan

SOFTWARE REQUIRED:

- Microsoft Word

The Company Description

THE TEEN ENTREPRENEUR

YOUR OBJECTIVE:

To produce the following section of your business plan:
• the Company Description

BACKGROUND INFORMATION BEFORE YOU BEGIN:

What is the Company Description Section of a Business Plan?

The **Company Description** section of a business plan provides the reader with a brief overview of the business including the business name and other relevant information about the business. The Company Description section is usually placed near the beginning of the business plan to establish a framework for the reader.

What's Included in the Company Description?

The Company Description section of a business plan usually includes the following components:

1. The company name
2. A general summary of the business
3. A declaration of a business form of ownership. Will the business be operated as a sole proprietorship, partnership, or corporation?
   Note: *Unless otherwise specified by your instructor, you will be required to declare your business as a sole proprietorship in this simulation.*
4. An industry classification for the business. This will be discussed in more detail in the "See It in Action with Shaun Decker" section later in this project.
5. The location of the business. In other words, where will the day-to-day operations of the business take place?
6. The year the business was formed

7. The primary function of the business. What are the main products or services provided by the business?
8. How many employees, if any, will be working for the company? What will their job titles be?
9. Who (if anyone) will be providing advice on legal, insurance, and accounting issues? These people are commonly referred to as "business advisors."

Creating a Name for Your Business

Above all things, the name of a business is probably the most important aspect to its success, yet it is usually dismissed as an unimportant step.

When considering a name for your business, follow the guidelines provided below.

A business name should:

1. convey an immediate impression of your business to customers.
2. convey expertise in the products and/or services being offered by your business.
3. convey the value and uniqueness of your products and/or services.
4. convey the qualities and benefits of your products and/or services.
5. convey the desired style and image of your business.
6. be pleasant and positive to read or hear.
7. be easy to pronounce.
8. be easy to remember.
9. be non-limiting to accommodate future growth and expansion of the business.
10. consist of no more than two or three words.

A business name should not:

1. deliberately contain misspelled words.
2. be too similar to other business names.
3. offend or embarrass potential customers.
4. be too vague or too general. For example, the business name "ACME" does not tell potential customers what business it is. Whereas, the name "ACME Movers" immediately lets the customer know it is a moving business.
5. begin with an article (A, An, The).
6. consist of more than three words.

Does the Business Name You Want Already Exist?

When selecting a business name, it is important that you determine if the business name is already in use by another business entity. Not only is it ethically wrong to use a business name that already exists, but most states have strict laws set up to protect the names of businesses. A good place to quickly check the availability of a business name is the United States Patent and Trademark Office (USPTO) Web site. The USPTO is a huge database provided by the Federal Government which includes every patent and trademark name currently in use in the United States. A **trademark** is a name, symbol, or other device identifying a product or business, officially registered and legally restricted to the use of the owner or manufacturer. Another place to check the availability of business names is with your state's Secretary of State department.

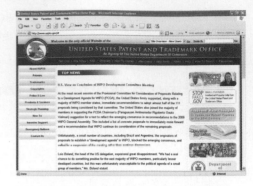

Search for business names you are considering at the United States Patent and Trademark Web site at *www.uspto.gov.*

Now let's learn how Shaun Decker created the Company Description section of his business plan

Shaun Decker's Company Description

Shaun already had the necessary information to complete some of the parts required in the "Company Description" section of his business plan. However, Shaun had to still create a name for his business and conduct some research in order to complete several of the other parts.

Creating a Business Name

Realizing the importance of choosing the right business name, Shaun researched the process of naming his desktop publishing business.

After a couple of hours of looking through the phone book and surfing the Internet for names of established desktop publishing enterprises, he came up with the following five possibilities:

> ## Possible Business Names:
> 1. Shaun Decker, Desktop Publishing Services
> 2. Decker's Publishing
> 3. Shaun's Publishing
> 4. Decker's Visual Communications
> 5. Decker's Digital Desktop

Shaun looked at his list of possible business names over and over again. He presented the list to his friends and family to get their opinions. Most of the people Shaun surveyed liked the sound of "Decker's Digital Desktop." They thought it made the name noteworthy and memorable.

Before making a final decision on his business name, Shaun wanted to make sure that his business name was not already being used by another company. Shaun logged on to the United States Patent and Trademark Office Web site (*www.uspto.gov*) and searched under "Trademarks" using his desired name of "Decker's Digital Desktop" (see Figure 2.1). The search yielded no results, indicating that the name "Decker's Digital Desktop" was not being used by any other business entity. He also checked with the New York Office of the Secretary of State and found

Figure 2.1

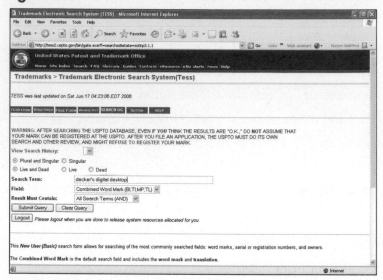

Shaun Decker used the United States Patent and Trademark Office Web site (*www.uspto.gov*) to determine if his desired business name was already in use.

that the name was not taken. At this point, it was safe for Shaun to use "Decker's Digital Desktop" for his business name.

Form of Ownership

Since Shaun was just getting started, he decided that operating the business by himself would be the best solution at this stage of the game. Therefore, Shaun declared his business as a sole proprietorship.

Industry Classification

Next, Shaun needed to obtain an industry classification for his desktop publishing business. Shaun used the Internet to find the North American Industry Classification System (NAICS) Web site (*www.naics.com*) to assist him. Using the search option, Shaun typed in "desktop publishing" and learned that the industry classification for a desktop publishing business was "Document Preparation Services" and the NAICS code number was "561410."

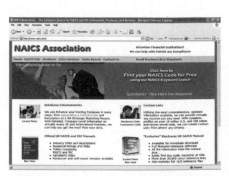

Shaun visited the North American Industry Classification System Web site (*www.naics.com*) to find the industry classification for his desktop publishing business.

Business Location

Shaun's logical choice was to operate his business from his home. Shaun wanted to be sure that operating the business from his home was in compliance with his local community zoning laws. **Zoning laws** are regulations that govern the type of use for a property within a community.

Shaun remembered learning about the Small Business Administration (SBA) in his Introduction to Business course. The SBA is a free service provided by the Federal Government to assist small businesses in getting established. After visiting and researching the SBA Web site (*www.sba.gov*), Shaun called his local city hall and spoke to a zoning officer, who informed him that his neighborhood was zoned residential and not for business (commercial) use. However, Shaun learned that he could obtain a **variance** (legal permission to use the property for another purpose) as long as his business would not create excessive customer traffic to the property. Since most of his transactions with customers would take place at the customers' locations, this would not create excessive traffic to Shaun's home.

All Shaun needed to do was to have his parents (the legal owners of the property) fill out a variance application and submit it for approval by the zoning board. Shaun filed the variance application and a few weeks later received approval from his local zoning board to operate the business from his parents' home.

With this step complete, Shaun was ready to write the "Company Description" of his business plan.

> Shaun Decker's completed "Company Description" section of his business plan is provided on the next page.

Shaun Decker's Company Description:

Company Description

I. Company Name

The legal business name is "Decker's Digital Desktop."

II. Business Summary

Decker's Digital Desktop is a desktop publishing business established to provide area businesses with desktop publishing services.

III. Form of Ownership

Decker's Digital Desktop will operate as a sole proprietorship. The proprietor of the business is Shaun Decker, the owner.

IV. Industry Classification

According to the North American Industry Classification System (NAICS), the industry classification for a desktop publishing business is "Document Preparation Service." The NAICS code number is 561410.

V. Location

Decker's Digital Desktop will operate from the owner's home residing at 123 Prescott Avenue in Pleasant Landing, NY.

VI. Year Established

Decker's Digital Desktop was established in 2006.

VII. Primary Function

The primary function of Decker's Digital Desktop will be to provide area businesses with desktop publishing services in the form of both print and electronic documents.

VIII. Employees

Shaun Decker, the owner, will be the only employee of Decker's Digital Desktop.

IX. Business Advisors

Jeff and Caroline Decker, the owner's parents, will serve as business advisors to Decker's Digital Desktop.

Now it's your turn to create the Company Description section of your business plan

Project 2:
Create the Company Description
Section of Your Business Plan

Follow the instructions provided below.

1. Using Microsoft Word, retrieve the file "Project2_Worksheet" from the "Teen Entrepreneur" folder installed from the Data CD.

2. Type your name and the current date in the header section of page 1 in the document.

3. Follow the instructions provided in the document to complete the worksheet.

4. Carefully proofread your work for accuracy and format.

5. Print a copy of the completed worksheet.

6. Save the completed worksheet to the "My Business Plan" folder.

7. Using Microsoft Word, open the file "Project2_Template" from the "Teen Entrepreneur" folder installed from the Data CD.

8. Complete all of the sections provided in the "Project2_Template" file to write the "Company Name and Description" section of your business plan. Use the "Overview" notes and Shaun Decker's "Company Name and Description" as a guide. *Tip: Copy and paste the answers that are relevant from the "Project2_Worksheet" file.*

9. Carefully proofread your work for accuracy and format.

10. Save the file as "Project2_Company_Description" to the "My Business Plan" folder.

11. Print a copy of the document.

MY
BUSINESS
PLAN

Project 3:
Creating a Logo
and Tagline

For Your Business Plan

Approximate Completion Time: 1–2 hours

Business Plan Checklist

INCLUDED IN THIS SECTION:

- Overview of Logos and Taglines
- See It In Action with Shaun Decker
- Now It's Your Turn to Build Your Business Plan

SOFTWARE REQUIRED:

- Drawing or illustration program such as Adobe Photoshop, Adobe Illustrator, or Microsoft Paint
- Adobe Acrobat Reader

Creating a Logo and Tagline

THE TEEN ENTREPRENEUR

YOUR OBJECTIVE:

To produce the following for your business plan:
- a Logo
- a Tagline

BACKGROUND INFORMATION BEFORE YOU BEGIN:

What is a Logo?

A **logo** is a name, symbol, or trademark designed for easy recognition. Logos can be made up of text only, or a combination of text and graphics. The goal of a logo is to always project the company's intended image.

Logos are used on just about every document a business produces including:
- Business cards
- Letterhead
- Advertisements and flyers
- Brochures
- Signs and posters

Logo Design Guidelines

When designing a logo for your business, follow the guidelines presented below.

1. Your logo should project your company's image.
2. Your logo design should be simple. Creating a logo with too many graphics or too much text makes it difficult to read and remember. You want to design a logo that customers will remember for the long-term.
3. Your logo should be unique, easily recognizable, and it should be different from your competitors.

4. If you will be using a color printer, keep the number of colors in your logo to a minimum. The colors you use in the logo will become the "signature" colors of your company.

Logos that Have Stood the Test of Time

Figure 3.1 shows some logos that have stood the test of time. Notice how each logo is simple to read, uses minimum colors, and includes the company name within the logo.

Figure 3.1

What is a Tagline?

A **tagline** is a repeated phrase or selection of words associated with a specific individual, organization, or product. Another word commonly used for a tagline is a slogan.

Taglines are the first step and an integral part of brand building. Their value builds for years, and over time, a good tagline can be your best and least expensive form of advertising. If your company name, logo, and tagline are all working together as they should, they become an advertisement in and of themselves. Refer to Table 3.1 to view some successful taglines that have stood the test of time.

No matter what your company does, your tagline creates a first impression. Sometimes people will remember a tagline even before the company name.

Successful taglines should:
1. be short and to the point.
2. consist of no more than four to six words.
3. convey a message of what your business provides.
4. be consistent with your logo design.
5. be easy to remember by potential customers.

Table 3.1

Taglines That Have Stood The Test of Time	
Tagline	**Product/Company**
When you care enough to send the very best.	Hallmark
Good to the last drop!	Maxwell House Coffee
mmm…mmm…good!	Campbell's
I'm lovin' it!	McDonald's
Drivers wanted.	Volkswagen
They're grrreeeaaat!	Kellogg's Sugar Frosted Flakes
Must see TV.	National Broadcasting Company (NBC)
Always low prices!	Wal-Mart
Have it your way.	Burger King
Pizza! Pizza!	Little Caesars
Like a rock.	Chevrolet
Do the "Dew".	Mountain Dew
Is IT in you?	Gatorade
Think outside the bun.	Taco Bell
Snap. Crackle. Pop.	Kellogg's Rice Crispies
Shift	Nissan
Once you pop, you can't stop!	Pringle's Potato Chips

Now let's learn how Shaun Decker created a Logo and Tagline for his business plan

Shaun Decker's Logo and Tagline

Shaun Decker now set upon the task of developing a logo and tagline for Decker's Digital Desktop.

For the tagline, Shaun created several catch phrases that would capture the essence of his desktop publishing business. After several revisions, Shaun decided on the tagline "*The Image of Your Future.*"

For his logo, Shaun wanted to create something that was simple, but that would also immediately grab the attention of potential customers. Since he was in the desktop publishing business, Shaun also wanted to include a graphic that conveyed a computer-related message.

Shaun began the logo design process by hand-sketching several possibilities on paper. Next, Shaun used a drawing software program to create five possible logos on the computer. He then printed the logos on one sheet of paper and surveyed his friends and family to get their opinions on the logo possibilities. He asked them to choose their favorite logo design from the following five possibilities:

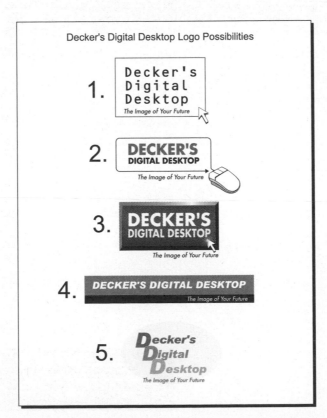

The results were unanimous. Nine out of the ten people Shaun surveyed picked logo #3. Shaun now had his logo and tagline secured.

With this step complete, Shaun was ready to add his company logo and tagline to his business plan.

Shaun Decker's completed logo and tagline for Decker's Digital Desktop is shown below.

Now it's your turn to create your company's Logo and Tagline for your business plan

Project 3:
Create a Logo and Tagline
for Your Business Plan

Follow the instructions provided below.

1. Open the file "Project3_Logo_Tagline_Planning_Form" from the "Teen Entrepreneur" folder installed from the Data CD. Print a copy of the document and follow the instructions provided. ***Note:*** *You will need Adobe Acrobat Reader to view and print this document.*

2. Using an illustration or drawing software program such as Adobe Illustrator, Adobe Photoshop, or Microsoft Paint, create your company logo. *Be sure that the tagline is visible somewhere in the logo.* Use the "Overview" notes and Shaun Decker's "Logo and Tagline" as a guide.

3. Save the logo as "Logo" in the "My Business Plan" folder.
   Note: *Save the logo in a format that will allow you to import it as a graphic image in Microsoft Word and Microsoft Publisher (.WMF, JPEG, TIFF, .BMP). The logo will be used in future projects.*

4. Print your logo.
   Keep the printout of your logo in a secure place as you will need to add it to your Business Plan at the conclusion of this simulation.

Real Teen Entrepreneur Success Story

Courtesy of Junior Achievement.

Ian Abston of Elkhart Lake, WI
Company: 2 Buff Guys

Ian Abston had only taken one business course while in high school. As it turns out, the experience made quite an impact on the Elkhart Lake High School student from Wisconsin. Ian was immediately inspired to start his own business!

"After the Junior Achievement Business Bowl, I started tracking stocks and bonds," claims Ian. "I also became interested in starting my own business."

The birth of "2 Buff Guys," a company specializing in lawn care and other handyman-type jobs soon followed. With large investments in advertising and promotions (business cards, flyers, "buff hours"), "2 Buff Guys" netted nearly $10,000 last summer alone! Ian and his partner have recently hired more workers to keep up with the demand, and have subcontracted with established landscaping businesses.

"The best thing about running my own business is the responsibility," says Ian. "I like being in charge."

Sounds like this "Buff" guy has brains and brawn—a compelling combination.

Project 4:
Creating the Description of Products and Services

Section of Your Business Plan

Approximate Completion Time: 1 hour

MY BUSINESS PLAN

Business Plan Checklist

✓ Project 1:   Choosing Your Teen-based Business
✓ Project 2:   Company Description
✓ Project 3:   Logo and Tagline
 Project 4:   Description of Products and Services
 Project 5:   Market Analysis
 Project 6:   Business Card
 Project 7:   Company Letterhead
 Project 8:   Marketing Plan
 Project 9:   Operating Plan
 Project 10: Schedule of Startup Funds Required
 Project 11: Customer Prospect Database
 Project 12: Introductory Promotional Letter
 Project 13: Three-Panel Brochure
 Project 14: Newspaper Advertisement
 Project 15: Owner's Resume
 Project 16: Projected Income Statement
 Project 17: Promotional Slide Show
 Project 18: Executive Summary
 Project 19: Business Plan Cover Page
 Project 20: Final Assembly of Your Business Plan
 Project 21: Company Web Site Homepage (*optional*)

INCLUDED IN THIS SECTION:

- Overview of the Description of Products and Services
- See It In Action with Shaun Decker
- Now It's Your Turn to Build Your Business Plan

SOFTWARE REQUIRED:

 - Microsoft Word

The Description of Products and Services

THE TEEN ENTREPRENEUR

To produce the following section of your business plan:
• the Description of Products and Services

What is the Description of Products and Services Section of a Business Plan?

Contrary to its title, the Description of Products and Services section of a business plan does not provide a list of products and services provided by the business preparing the plan. Rather, the **Description of Products and Services** section of a business plan includes general information about the industry the business will be involved in. Its purpose is to familiarize the reader of the business plan with the industry the business will be operating in.

What's Included in the Description of Products and Services?

The Description of Products and Services section of a business plan usually includes the following items:

1. **Description of the Industry**
   • What is the definition of the industry?
   • What is the general purpose of this type of industry?
   • What is the general nature of the type of work performed in this type of industry?

2. **Products and/or Services Provided**
   • What type of product(s) and/or service(s) does this type of business provide?

3. **Nature of the Work**
   • How are the product(s) and/or service(s) produced in this type of business?

Why Include a Description of the Products and Services in a Business Plan?

Including a Description of Products and Services in a business plan serves two purposes:

1. It allows the owner of the business to become more familiar with the industry he or she will be doing business in.
2. It educates readers of your business plan who may not be familiar with your type of business.

Writing the Description of Products and Services

When writing the Description of Products and Services section of a business plan, the information provided should be specific and detailed, but not too technical. It is important that the reader, especially those not familiar with the type of business, clearly understands the Description of the Products and Services.

Now let's learn how Shaun Decker created the Description of Products and Services section of his business plan

Shaun Decker's
Description of Products and Services

To begin writing the "Description of Products and Services" section of his business plan, Shaun decided that it would be useful to research the desktop publishing industry to see what products and services they provide. He also wanted to look at some of the other businesses that provide a similar service, also known as the **competition**.

With this step complete, Shaun was ready to write the "Description of Products and Services" section of his business plan.

Shaun Decker's completed "Description of Products and Services" section of his business plan is provided on the next page.

Shaun Decker's Description of Products and Services:

Description of Products and Services

I. Description of the Industry

Desktop publishing is the design and production of publications using personal computers with graphics capability. Desktop publishers produce professional print documents and professional electronic documents using a personal computer, desktop publishing software, a digital camera, a scanner, and a color printer. Desktop publishers help produce a variety of documents necessary to the day-to-day operations of businesses.

II. Products and/or Services Provided

Desktop publishers provide the expertise to produce all or some of the following print and electronic documents:

letterhead	newsletters	reports
envelopes	business forms	proposals
business cards	books	calendars
flyers	menus	resumes
print ads	signs	greeting cards
brochures	gift certificates	bumper stickers
catalogs	awards	iron-on transfers
manuals	posters	presentations
directories	tickets	Web pages/Web sites

III. Nature of the work

The services provided by a desktop publisher include all or some of the following to produce a finished product:

1. Format and combine text, numerical data, photographs, charts, and other visual and graphic elements to produce publication-ready material
2. Write and/or edit text
3. Convert photos/drawings into digital images and then manipulate those images
4. Design page layouts
5. Publish the final project to paper or electronic media

> Now it's your turn to create your
> **Description of Products and Services**
> section of your business plan

Project 4:
Create the Description of Products and Services Section of Your Business Plan

Follow the instructions provided below.

1. Using Microsoft Word, retrieve the file "Project4_Worksheet" from the "Teen Entrepreneur" folder installed from the Data CD.
2. Type your name and the current date in the header section of page 1 in the document.
3. Follow the instructions provided in the document to complete the worksheet.
4. Carefully proofread your work for accuracy and format.
5. Print a copy of the completed worksheet.
6. Save the completed worksheet to the "My Business Plan" folder.
7. Using Microsoft Word, open the file "Project4_Template" from the "Teen Entrepreneur" folder installed from the Data CD.
8. Complete all of the sections provided in the "Project4_Template" file to write the "Description of Products and Services" section of your business plan. Use the "Overview" notes and Shaun Decker's "Description of Products and Services" as a guide. *Tip: Copy and paste the answers that are relevant from the "Project4_Worksheet" file.*
9. Carefully proofread your work for accuracy and format.
10. Save the file as "Project4_Products_Services" to the "My Business Plan" folder.
11. Print a copy of the document.

Project 5: Creating the Market Analysis

Section of Your Business Plan

Approximate Completion Time: 1–1.5 hours

Business Plan Checklist

- ✓ Project 1: Choosing Your Teen-based Business
- ✓ Project 2: Company Description
- ✓ Project 3: Logo and Tagline
- ✓ Project 4: Description of Products and Services
- Project 5: Market Analysis
- Project 6: Business Card
- Project 7: Company Letterhead
- Project 8: Marketing Plan
- Project 9: Operating Plan
- Project 10: Schedule of Startup Funds Required
- Project 11: Customer Prospect Database
- Project 12: Introductory Promotional Letter
- Project 13: Three-Panel Brochure
- Project 14: Newspaper Advertisement
- Project 15: Owner's Resume
- Project 16: Projected Income Statement
- Project 17: Promotional Slide Show
- Project 18: Executive Summary
- Project 19: Business Plan Cover Page
- Project 20: Final Assembly of Your Business Plan
- Project 21: Company Web Site Homepage (*optional*)

INCLUDED IN THIS SECTION:

- Overview of the Market Analysis
- See It In Action with Shaun Decker
- Now It's Your Turn to Build Your Business Plan

SOFTWARE REQUIRED:

- Microsoft Word

The Market Analysis

THE TEEN ENTREPRENEUR

YOUR OBJECTIVE:

To produce the following section of your business plan:
- the Market Analysis

BACKGROUND INFORMATION BEFORE YOU BEGIN:

What is a Market Analysis?

Imagine practicing archery with your eyes closed or throwing a football with a blindfold on. In both cases, being prevented from seeing your target would make it nearly impossible to hit it. This concept can easily be applied to business as well. Doing business without knowing who your target market is will prevent you from reaching your objective of making a profit.

A **market analysis** is the actual assessment of the target population, competition, and needs for marketing a product or service.

Why Include a Market Analysis in a Business Plan?

Conducting a market analysis is the first step in determining if there is a need or audience for your business. Knowing the market's needs and how it is currently serviced can provide you with key information that is essential in developing your business and the products and/or services you offer. Too often, new businesses spend thousands of dollars on startup costs without first researching the market and the competition. To be successful, it is critical that you conduct a market analysis and include one in your business plan.

Four Components of a Market Analysis

While the format can vary from industry to industry, there are several standard components to include in the Market Analysis section of a business plan.

A good market analysis should include the following four components:

1. Analysis of the Target Market

In developing the analysis of the target market, you should answer the following questions:

- *Who is my target market and why? In other words, who are my customers?*
- *What are the personal and geographical demographics of my customers?*

    Personal demographics include identifying factors such as age, gender, sex, and income of the target market.

    Geographical demographics include identifying factors such as city or town location, population, and climate.
- Are my customers businesses or private consumers?
- Is the market saturated or wide open? In other words, are there too many businesses like mine in the same area?
- Are customers willing to pay for my product(s) and/or service(s)?

2. Analysis of the Competition

In developing the analysis of the competition, you should answer the following questions:

- *Who is my competition?*
- *Are my competitors successful?*
- *How do my competitors reach their market? In other words, how is the competition advertising their businesses?*

3. The Outlook of the Industry

In developing the analysis of the outlook of the industry, you should answer the following questions:

- *What does the future outlook of my business look like?*
- *Is it a growing industry? Or is this industry likely to be phased out over time?*

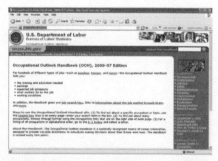

A good resource to research the future outlook of your industry is the **OOH (Occupational Outlook Handbook)** Web site (*www.bls.gov/oco*), provided by the U.S. Bureau of Labor Statistics. The OOH is a free online service that can provide prospective entrepreneurs and job seekers with a wealth of useful knowledge about the outlook of a specific career or business. On the Web site, click on the "A-Z Index" and then search on a job title that closely relates to the nature of your business. Once you have located your target job title, look under the category of "Job Outlook." You will find a detailed analysis of the future of this career. If the employment of this career is expected to grow, you can assume that your business should be able to compete successfully in your market.

4. The Owner's Personal Strengths

In developing the analysis of the owner's personal strengths, you should answer the following questions:

- *What is my competitive advantage?*
- *Can I offer something to the market that my competitors are not offering?*
- *What specific skills do I possess that will allow my company to be competitive in this market?*

Now let's learn how Shaun Decker created the Market Analysis section of his business plan

Shaun Decker's Market Analysis

Shaun knew the importance of conducting a market analysis. Shaun is a go-getter and wanted to be sure that his desktop publishing business would be a success. He was eager to find out more about his target market and knew that, to be competitive, he would need to research his competition thoroughly.

The Target Market

Since Shaun will be targeting small businesses as customers for his business, he visited his local Chamber of Commerce to find out if there was a growth or decline in new businesses formed in his community.

The Competition

To find out more about his competition, Shaun used the local telephone book to research other businesses in his community that offer desktop publishing services.

The Outlook of the Industry

Shaun used the Occupational Outlook Handbook Web site to find out more about the future outlook of the desktop publishing industry.

With these steps complete, Shaun was ready to create the "Market Analysis" section of his business plan.

> Shaun Decker's completed "Market Analysis" section of his business plan is provided on the next two pages.

Shaun Decker's Market Analysis:

Market Analysis

I. Analysis of the Target Market

While realizing that people from all walks of life could at one time or another use the services of a desktop publisher, the target market will be small businesses.

Rationale: Small businesses often do not have the need or funds to have a full-time desktop publisher. Therefore, they will need to seek their desktop publishing needs from an outside source. Furthermore, small businesses would also be likely to purchase paper products (business cards, brochures, etc.) in smaller quantities; orders larger publishing houses would likely prefer not to handle. This creates a good market niche for Decker's Digital Desktop!

Research conducted at the local Chamber of Commerce indicated that small businesses are on the rise in the Pleasant Landing, New York area. Therefore, there appears to be a steady future growth and need for desktop publishing services.

II. Analysis of the Competition

A search of the regional telephone directory and the business directory of the local Chamber of Commerce yielded the following competitors in the desktop publishing category:

> The Printed Page
> Paper Stocks
> Noffri's Publishing
> Electronic Publishers, Inc.

Only one competitor, Electronic Publishers, had a Web presence, which indicates that the other competitors were most likely very small publishing houses dealing in primarily paper products. Based on discussions with local businesses, it appears that the chief competitor to Decker's Digital Desktop is Electronic Publishers. It should be noted, however, that Electronic Publishers' corporate information page leads the owner to believe that the company targets primarily large businesses, whereas Decker's Digital Desktop will focus primarily on small businesses.

III. The Outlook of the Industry

After visiting the Occupational Outlook Handbook Web site, the following information was derived regarding the future outlook for desktop publishers:

1

Shaun Decker's Market Analysis continued:

> Employment of desktop publishers is expected to grow faster than average for all occupations through 2014, as more page layout and design work is performed in-house using computers and sophisticated publishing software. Many new jobs for desktop publishers are expected to emerge in commercial printing and publishing establishments. In addition to employment growth, many job openings for desktop publishers also will result from the need to replace workers who move into managerial positions, transfer to other occupations, or leave the labor force.
>
> Printing and publishing costs represent a significant portion of a corporation's expenses, and firms are finding it more profitable to print their own newsletters and other reports than to send them out to trade shops. Desktop publishing reduces the time needed to complete a printing job and allows commercial printers to make inroads into new markets that require fast turnaround.
>
> Most employers prefer to hire experienced desktop publishers. As more people gain desktop publishing experience, however, competition for jobs may increase. Among persons without experience, opportunities should be best for those with computer backgrounds who are certified or who have completed postsecondary programs in desktop publishing or graphic design. Many employers prefer graduates of these programs because the comprehensive training they receive helps them learn the page layout process and adapt more rapidly to new software and techniques.

While the research provided by the Occupational Outlook Handbook Web site states that "firms are finding it more profitable to print their own newsletters and other reports than to send them out to trade shops...," Decker's Digital Desktop will be an asset to the small business owner who cannot afford to hire full-time desktop publishing staff. Therefore, it is concluded that the outlook for the desktop publishing industry is strong and growing.

IV. Owner's Personal Strengths

Since Decker's Digital Desktop will operate out of the owner's parents' residence, overhead expenses required to run the business will be minimal. The savings in overhead expenses will be passed on to the customer, offering a competitive advantage.

2

Now it's your turn to create the Market Analysis section of your business plan

Project 5:
Create the Market Analysis Section
of Your Business Plan

Follow the instructions provided below.

1. Using Microsoft Word, retrieve the file "Project5_Worksheet" from the "Teen Entrepreneur" folder installed from the Data CD.
2. Type your name and the current date in the header section of page 1 in the document.
3. Follow the instructions provided in the document to complete the worksheet.
4. Carefully proofread your work for accuracy and format.
5. Print a copy of the completed worksheet.
6. Save the completed worksheet to the "My Business Plan" folder.
7. Using Microsoft Word, open the file "Project5_Template" from the "Teen Entrepreneur" folder installed from the Data CD.
8. Complete all of the sections provided in the "Project5_Template" file to write the "Market Analysis" section of your business plan. Use the "Overview" notes and Shaun Decker's "Market Analysis" as a guide.
   Tip: Copy and paste the answers that are relevant from the "Project5_Worksheet" file.
9. Carefully proofread your work for accuracy and format.
10. Save the file as "Project5_Market_Analysis" to the "My Business Plan" folder.
11. Print a copy of the document.

Courtesy of Junior Achievement.

Brian Hendricks of Potomac, MD
Company: StartUpPC.com

Brian Hendricks is a 17-year-old student, computer whiz, and entrepreneur from Potomac, Maryland.

Brian knew at a very young age that he had a talent for building and fixing computers. What began as a project spawned from frustration ("I was fed up with my slow, boring, and unoriginal computer made by a large company," says Brian.) soon turned into the successful business it is today.

Today, Brian's PC business, StartUpPC.com, specializes not only in computer repair, but also the custom-creation of computers to suit the exact needs of the client.

Earning nearly $2,500 a month through StartUpPC.com, Brian has a fool-proof strategy for running his business: "Instead of setting huge goals and putting every last penny in your pocket to reach them, I believe in starting small and just not giving up," says Brian.

Brian was named Junior Achievement's 2005 Student Entrepreneur of the Year.

Project 6: Creating a Business Card

For Your Business Plan

Approximate Completion Time: 1 hour

MY BUSINESS PLAN

Business Plan Checklist

✓ Project 1: Choosing Your Teen-based Business
✓ Project 2: Company Description
✓ Project 3: Logo and Tagline
✓ Project 4: Description of Products and Services
✓ Project 5: Market Analysis
   Project 6: Business Card
   Project 7: Company Letterhead
   Project 8: Marketing Plan
   Project 9: Operating Plan
   Project 10: Schedule of Startup Funds Required
   Project 11: Customer Prospect Database
   Project 12: Introductory Promotional Letter
   Project 13: Three-Panel Brochure
   Project 14: Newspaper Advertisement
   Project 15: Owner's Resume
   Project 16: Projected Income Statement
   Project 17: Promotional Slide Show
   Project 18: Executive Summary
   Project 19: Business Plan Cover Page
   Project 20: Final Assembly of Your Business Plan
   Project 21: Company Web Site Homepage (*optional*)

INCLUDED IN THIS SECTION:

- Overview of the Business Card
- See It In Action with Shaun Decker
- Now It's Your Turn to Build Your Business Plan

SOFTWARE REQUIRED:

- Microsoft Word, Microsoft Publisher, or Any Desktop Publishing Software
- Adobe Acrobat Reader

The Business Card

THE TEEN ENTREPRENEUR

YOUR OBJECTIVE:

To produce the following item to be included in your business plan:
- an Owner's Business Card

BACKGROUND INFORMATION BEFORE YOU BEGIN:

What is a Business Card and Why Have One?

A **business card** is a small card printed or engraved with a person's name and business affiliation, including such information as job title, address, e-mail address, Web site address, and telephone and fax numbers. The purpose of a business card is to announce one's identity, presence, and the intention to conduct business. The business card is perhaps the most widely used mini-document in the business world. Simply said, the business card is the handshake you leave behind after meeting someone in the professional world.

What to Include on a Business Card

Business cards usually contain the following elements:

1. Business name
2. Postal mailing address
3. Telephone and fax numbers
4. Web site address (URL)
5. The business logo and tagline
6. Name and job title of the individual representing the business
7. E-mail address of the individual representing the business
8. Sometimes an additional graphic image
9. Brief list of products and/or services offered by the business

Business Card Layout and Design Guidelines

The importance of a business card cannot be stressed enough when it comes to projecting a professional and long-lasting image in the minds of potential and existing customers.

When designing the layout of the business card, consider the following tips and guidelines:

1. **Information.** Decide what information should go on the business card. Remember, you want the reader to remember who you are, what you do, and how to contact you.

2. **Do Not Overcrowd.** Since the business card is a very small document, it is important not to try and "squeeze" too much information on it. You do not want to lose the most important information on the card due to overcrowding.

3. **Consistency.** The look and design of a business card should be consistent with other documents used in the business. This helps to project a professional image. It says, "I care about the way you perceive me and my business."

4. **Typefaces (Fonts).** Use no more than two different typefaces (fonts) on your business card. This helps create a clean, easy-to-read business card.

5. **Proportion.** Keep the size and placement of each element on the business card balanced and in proportion. This will help make the card more pleasing on the eyes of the reader.

6. **Have a Paper Plan.** Before putting anything on the computer, sketch several possible business cards on paper and experiment with different layouts and designs.

Why Include a Business Card in a Business Plan?

Including a business card in a business plan does two things:

1. It projects a level of professionalism for the owner of the business.
2. It helps give the reader of the business plan a clear image of the company's identity and image.

If included, a business card is usually put as a supplemental attachment or in the appendix in a business plan.

Now let's look at the Business Card Shaun Decker created for his business plan

Shaun Decker's Business Card

As the owner of a desktop publishing business, Shaun knew that his business card would reflect the quality of the work that potential customers could expect from him in designing publications for their business. As such, Shaun's business card could make or break a potential sale.

After a great deal of thought and plenty of layout and text changes, Shaun was ready to create his business card which he would add as a supplemental attachment to his business plan.

Shaun Decker's business card is provided below.

DECKER'S DIGITAL DESKTOP
The Image of Your Future

Desktop Publishing • Web Development

Shaun Decker, Owner
123 Prescott Ave • Pleasant Landing, NY 19999
Phone: (315) 999-9797 • www.DeckersDigitalDesktop.com

Note: Although Shaun did not have a Web site developed at this stage in his business, he did plan to create one. He did research on the Internet and found that the domain name "DeckersDigitalDesktop.com" was available. Therefore, he added the Web site address to his business card. You will learn more about Shaun Decker's Web site later in this simulation.

Now it's your turn to create a
Business Card for your business plan

Project 6:
Create a Business Card for Your Business Plan

Follow the instructions provided below.

1. Open the file "Project6_Business_Card_Planning_Form" from the "Teen Entrepreneur" folder installed from the Data CD. Print a copy of the document and follow the instructions provided. *Note: You will need Adobe Acrobat Reader to view and print this document.*

2. Using Microsoft Word, Microsoft Publisher, or any desktop publishing software, create a new document.

3. Draw a bordered frame measuring 3.5 inches wide by 2 inches high (*the size of a standard business card*). Place this frame in the center of the document.

4. Place the contents of your business card within the rectangle border. *Note: Be sure to use the logo you created in Project 3 in your business card.* Use the "Overview" notes and Shuan Decker's "Business Card" as a guide.

5. Carefully proofread your work for accuracy and format.

6. Save the file as "Project6_Biz_Card" to the "My Business Plan" folder.

7. Print a copy of the document.

   Keep the document in a secure place as you will need to add it to your Business Plan at the conclusion of this simulation.

Project 7: Creating Company Letterhead

For Your Business Plan

Approximate Completion Time: .5 hours

LETTERHEAD

Business Plan Checklist

INCLUDED IN THIS SECTION:

- Overview of Company Letterhead
- See It In Action with Shaun Decker
- Now It's Your Turn to Build Your Business Plan

SOFTWARE REQUIRED:

- Microsoft Word
- Adobe Acrobat Reader

Company Letterhead

THE TEEN ENTREPRENEUR

YOUR OBJECTIVE:

To produce the following item to be included in your business plan:
• Company Letterhead

BACKGROUND INFORMATION BEFORE YOU BEGIN:

What is Company Letterhead and Why Have It?

Company letterhead is the heading that is printed at the top of a sheet of letter size paper, usually consisting of a company name, logo, address, Web site address, and telephone and fax numbers. Letterhead is similar to a business card in that it provides the reader with important contact information about a business.

Businesses usually send correspondence to their customers and vendors to project a professional image and to remind the reader of where the correspondence originated.

Letterhead is usually preprinted or inserted in the first 2 to 2.5 inches of space in the top margin of the first page of a document. Some companies place some or all parts of their letterhead in the left, right, or bottom margin(s).

What to Include in the Letterhead

The following elements are usually included in the letterhead of a document:

1. The company's name
2. The company's logo and tagline
3. The company's address
4. The company's telephone and fax numbers
5. The company's Web site address (if applicable)

Letterhead Layout and Design

Refer to the layout and design tips provided in Project 6 for business cards before designing the layout of your letterhead. Remember that consistency is the key in promoting your business, so the layout, design, and style of your letterhead should be similar to your business card.

Why Include Company Letterhead in a Business Plan?

Like the business card, including a sample of company letterhead in a business plan does two things:

1. It projects a level of professionalism for the owner of the business.
2. It helps give the reader of the business plan a clear image of the company's identity and image.

If included, company letterhead is usually put as a supplemental attachment or in the appendix in a business plan.

Now let's look at the Company Letterhead Shaun Decker created for his business plan

Shaun Decker's Company Letterhead

Realizing the importance of projecting a professional, consistent business image, Shaun wanted his company letterhead to match the look and design of his business card. After experimenting with several designs, Shaun was ready to create his company letterhead which he planned to add as a supplemental attachment to his business plan.

> Shaun Decker's company letterhead is provided below.

DECKER'S DIGITAL DESKTOP
The Image of Your Future

Shaun Decker, Owner
123 Prescott Ave • Pleasant Landing, NY 19999
Phone: (315) 999-9797 • www.DeckersDigitalDesktop.com

Desktop Publishing • Web Development

> **Now it's your turn to create the Company Letterhead for your business plan**

Project 7:
Create Company Letterhead
for Your Business Plan

Follow the instructions provided below.

1. Open the file "Project7_Letterhead_Planning_Form" from the "Teen Entrepreneur" folder installed from the Data CD. Print a copy of the document and follow the instructions provided. *Note: You will need Adobe Acrobat Reader to view and print this document.*

2. Using Microsoft Word, create a new document.

3. Set the top page margin to 2 or 2.5 inches.

4. Place the contents of your letterhead in the top header section of your document. *Note: Be sure to use the logo you created in Project 3 in your letterhead.* Use the "Overview" notes and Shaun Decker's "Company Letterhead" as a guide.

5. Carefully proofread your work for accuracy and format.

6. Save the file as "Project7_Letterhead" to the "My Business Plan" folder.

7. Print a copy of the document.

   Keep the document in a secure place as you will need to add it to your Business Plan at the conclusion of this simulation.

Project 8: Creating the Marketing Plan

Section of Your Business Plan

Approximate Completion Time: 1 hour

My Marketing Plan

INCLUDED IN THIS SECTION:

- Overview of the Marketing Plan
- See It In Action with Shaun Decker
- Now It's Your Turn to Build Your Business Plan

SOFTWARE REQUIRED:

- Microsoft Word

Business Plan Checklist

The Marketing Plan

THE TEEN ENTREPRENEUR

To produce the following section of your business plan:
- the Marketing Plan

BACKGROUND INFORMATION BEFORE YOU BEGIN:

What is Marketing and Why Have a Marketing Plan?

Marketing is the activities of a company associated with buying and selling a product or service. It includes advertising, selling, and delivering products to people.

In order to successfully market and sell your products and/or services to customers, it is necessary to have a marketing plan. A **Marketing Plan** should address the 4 P's of Marketing, known as the marketing mix.

The 4 P's of Marketing are:
1. Product
2. Place
3. Price
4. Promotion

Each of the 4 P's of marketing is discussed in more detail below.

The 4 P's of the Marketing Plan

1. Product

In your Marketing Plan, you will have to answer this question: *What products will I sell?*

To answer this question, it is important to research the competition. In order to be competitive, a business needs to offer products that customers have already demonstrated a need for. The owner needs to evaluate what the business is capable of offering. For instance, let's say you are operating your own pet-walking business. As the owner, you have to evaluate when you are available to walk pets. If you are a full-time student, it would obviously not make sense to offer your services during school hours.

2. Place

In your Marketing Plan, you will have to answer this question: *Where will the products and/or services you sell be sold?*

To answer this question, you will have to evaluate your ability to travel to customer's locations, if applicable. *Will you operate your business from your home?*

3. Price

In your Marketing Plan, you will have to answer this question: *What price will I charge for the product(s) and/or service(s) I offer?*

To answer this question, you will have to conduct a cost analysis to determine the selling price of your product(s) and/or service(s). If you are providing a service-based only business, such as landscaping or hairstyling, you need to ask yourself how much money you would like to make per hour.

A careful study of your competitor's prices will allow you to set fair prices. You don't want to charge too much or your customers will look elsewhere. On the other hand, you don't want to charge too low of a price or customers may perceive your products and/or services as "cheap" and/or low quality.

4. Promotion

In your Marketing Plan, you will have to answer this question: *How will I promote and advertise the product(s) and/or service(s) I offer?*

To answer this question, you will have to once again look at what your competition is doing to advertise their products and/or services. There are literally hundreds of methods you can use to promote and advertise your business.

Some examples are:
- Flyers or sell sheets
- Print advertisements
- Brochures or pamphlets
- Business cards
- E-mail newsletters
- Web sites
- Billboards
- Direct mail

Careful research will tell you how much advertising will cost. You will have to look at how much money you have available and set your advertising goals and milestones accordingly. Do not get discouraged if at startup you do not have adequate funds available to advertise. Good business owners reinvest their profits into their businesses and use the money to grow the business steadily over time.

Now let's learn how Shaun Decker created the Marketing Plan section of his business plan

Shaun Decker's Marketing Plan

To complete the "Marketing Plan" section of the business plan, Shaun followed the 4 P's of the marketing mix (product, place, price, and promotion). What follows is an overview of how Shaun went about creating the marketing plan for Decker's Digital Desktop.

1. Product

To determine exactly what products he would offer to his customers, Shaun decided that his best resource was his competition. After shopping the competition, Shaun determined that only one of his local competitors offered electronic development services for Web site and presentation development. Since Shaun had a good deal of knowledge in building Web sites and creating computer presentations, he would definitely offer these two services. After conducting more research, Shaun determined that Decker's Digital Desktop would offer the following products and services:

1. Business Cards
2. Letterhead
3. Brochures
4. Presentation Development
5. Web Site Development
6. Word Processing Services

Shaun established a future goal to offer more products and services over time as the business grows.

2. Place (Location)

Since Shaun had permission from his parents and his town, he would conduct the development side of his business out of his parents' home. Since Shaun was old enough to drive, his parents also gave him permission to use the family car to travel to customers' locations. However, Shaun's parents were not comfortable with him traveling long distances and limited Shaun to traveling within the limits of his hometown.

3. Price

Before Shaun could set any selling prices for the products and services he offered, he needed to determine the cost of materials that would be necessary to produce the products he would be selling.

Researching online sources for paper products, ink, and toner, Shaun estimated the cost of materials as follows:

Product	Cost
Business Card	$0.02 each
Letterhead	$0.01 each
Brochures	$0.11 each

Having no prior experience in the desktop publishing business, Shaun once again turned to his competitors to determine his selling prices.

Shopping the competition produced the following information on average charges for products and services:

Product/Service	The Printed Page	Noffri's	Paper Stocks	Electronic Publishers
Business Cards (priced per 500 cards)	$80.00	$80.00	$85.00	$90.00
Brochures (priced per 200 brochures)	$110.00	$150.00	$160.00	$160.00
Letterhead (priced per 500 sheets)	$90.00	$95.00	$95.00	$110.00
Web Site Development (per hour)	N/A	N/A	N/A	$150.00
Presentation Development (per hour)	N/A	N/A	N/A	$100.00
Word Processing (per page)	$5.50	$5.00	N/A	N/A

Based on his research and evaluation of the competition, Shaun was confident that he could compete in the market and attract customers. As a home-based business, the operating costs for Decker's Digital Desktop would be less expensive, allowing Shaun to offer lower prices than his competitors.

Shaun set the pricing structure for Decker's Digital Desktop as follows:

Business Cards (priced per 500 cards)	$75.00
Brochures (priced per 200 brochures)	$105.00
Letterhead (priced per 500 sheets)	$85.00
Web Site Development	$50.00 per hour
Presentation Development	$30.00 per hour
Word Processing	$4.50 per page

4. Promotion

Shaun knew that in order to compete in the market, he would have to advertise his new business. While sitting at his desk at home, Shaun came up with the following list of possible ways to advertise Decker's Digital Desktop:

Possible Advertising Methods:

Local newspaper ad

Distribute flyers to local businesses

Local TV commercial

Local radio ad

Business cards

Brochures

Web site

Direct mail

Shaun knew that he could produce the flyers, business cards, brochures, Web site, and direct mail piece on his own premises for minimal cost. However, before making any decisions to advertise using the other methods he considered, Shaun conducted research to find out what they would cost. Shaun's research yielded the following comparisons:

Advertising Method	Cost
Local Newspaper ad (5 inches by 7 inches)	$100.00 (ad runs for 1 week)
Radio Ad (three 30-second spots for one day)	$350.00
Local TV Commercial (two 30-second spots for one day)	$500.00
Cost of postal stamp (for direct mail)	$0.39 each

Since Shaun had limited startup funds, he decided to advertise using the following methods:

1. Distribute brochures, promotional letters, and/or business cards to local businesses (either in person or by direct mail)
2. Local newspaper advertisement
3. Promotional slide show presentation

After initiating these advertising efforts, Shaun will evaluate their success and create another advertising plan in the future accordingly.

With the necessary background research finished, Shaun was ready to complete the "Marketing Plan" section of his business plan.

> Shaun Decker's completed "Marketing Plan" section of his business plan is provided on the next page.

Shaun Decker's Marketing Plan:

Marketing Plan

I. Product

Decker's Digital Desktop will offer the following products and services:

1. Business Cards
2. Letterhead
3. Brochures
4. Web Site Development
5. Presentation Development
6. Word Processing Services

II. Place

Day-to-day operations of the business will be conducted as follows:

1. Product development will be conducted at the owner's residence located at 123 Prescott Avenue, Pleasant Landing, NY 19999
2. Meetings and product delivery will be conducted at the customer's location. The customer base will be within the Pleasant Landing city limits.

III. Price

Decker's Digital Desktop pricing structure is as follows:

Business Cards (priced per 500 cards)	$75.00
Brochures (priced per 200 brochures)	$105.00
Letterhead (priced per 500 sheets)	$85.00
Web Site Development	$50.00 per hour
Presentation Development	$30.00 per hour
Word Processing	$4.50 per page

IV. Promotion

Decker's Digital Desktop will use the following advertising methods:

1. Distribute brochures, promotional letters, and/or business cards to local businesses in the Pleasant Landing area (either in person or by direct mail)
2. Local newspaper advertisement
3. Promotional slide show presentation

Now it's your turn to create the Marketing Plan section of your business plan

Project 8:
Create the Marketing Plan Section
of Your Business Plan

Follow the instructions provided below.

1. Using Microsoft Word, retrieve the file "Project8_Worksheet" from the "Teen Entrepreneur" folder installed from the Data CD.
2. Type your name and the current date in the header section of page 1 in the document.
3. Follow the instructions provided in the document to complete the worksheet.
4. Carefully proofread your work for accuracy and format.
5. Print a copy of the completed worksheet.
6. Save the completed worksheet to the "My Business Plan" folder.
7. Using Microsoft Word, open the file "Project8_Template" from the "Teen Entrepreneur" folder installed from the Data CD.
8. Complete all of the sections provided in the "Project8_Template" file to write the "Marketing Plan" section of your business plan. Use the "Overview" notes and Shaun Decker's "Marketing Plan" as a guide.
   Tip: Copy and paste the answers that are relevant from the "Project8_Worksheet" file.
9. Carefully proofread your work for accuracy and format.
10. Save the file as "Project8_Marketing_Plan" to the "My Business Plan" folder.
11. Print a copy of the document.

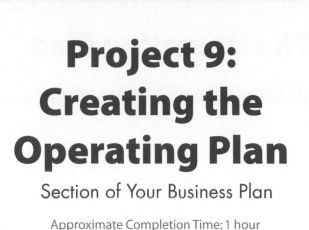

Project 9: Creating the Operating Plan

Section of Your Business Plan

Approximate Completion Time: 1 hour

Business Plan Checklist

INCLUDED IN THIS SECTION:

- Overview of the Operating Plan
- See It In Action with Shaun Decker
- Now It's Your Turn to Build Your Business Plan

SOFTWARE REQUIRED:

- Microsoft Word

The Operating Plan

THE TEEN ENTREPRENEUR

YOUR OBJECTIVE:

To produce the following section of your business plan:
- the Operating Plan

BACKGROUND INFORMATION BEFORE YOU BEGIN:

What is an Operating Plan and Why Have One?

The **Operating Plan** (also referred to as the business operations plan) section of a business plan should outline and describe the day-to-day operations of a business. One of the key elements included in an Operating Plan is to describe how the products and/or services offered by a business will be produced and delivered. An Operating Plan also allows businesses to analyze how much time will be devoted to other required daily tasks such as marketing and accounting practices.

An Operating Plan provides three key benefits to businesses:

1. It requires the business to analyze and research how to produce products and/or services using the most cost-effective manner—allowing the business to maximize profits.

2. It requires the business to analyze and research how to get goods and services to the customer using the most cost-effective manner—again, allowing the business to maximize profits.

3. It requires businesses to effectively time manage each task required to keep the business running.

What's Included in an Operating Plan?

While an Operating Plan can vary based on the type of business, it usually includes the following five categories:

1. Purchasing
2. Production
3. Sales and Marketing
4. Accounting
5. Distribution

Each of the five categories included in an Operating Plan is briefly discussed below.

The Five Categories Included in an Operating Plan

1. Purchasing

In your Operating Plan, you will have to answer the following questions:

• *What supplies and materials do I need to produce my products and/or services?*

• *Who are the best suppliers to provide the materials and supplies required for my business to produce the products and/or services? In other words, what suppliers provide the best prices, quality, and delivery time?*

2. Production

In your Operating Plan, you will have to answer the following question:

• *What is the production time required to complete a customer order from order receipt to delivery?*

3. Sales and Marketing

In your Operating Plan, you will have to answer the following question:

• *How much time each month will you spend on marketing and promoting your business?*

4. Accounting

In your Operating Plan, you will have to answer the following questions:

• *How will I keep accurate accounting records for my business?*

• *How much time will it take to conduct accounting tasks for my business?*

5. Distribution

In your Operating Plan, you will have to answer the following questions:

• *How much time will it take me to deliver products and/or services to the customer?*

• *How will I deliver the products and/or services?*

Now let's learn how Shaun Decker created the Operating Plan section of his business plan

Shaun Decker's Operating Plan

Shaun Decker's next step was to create the "Operating Plan" section of his business plan. What follows is an overview of how Shaun went about creating the "Operating Plan" for Decker's Digital Desktop.

1. Purchasing

To complete the purchasing section of the operating plan, Shaun used the Internet and local phone book to research the best suppliers for his company. He wanted to find suppliers who were reputable and quality conscious, while offering competitive prices.

2. Production

Shaun estimated that it would take approximately 2-4 days to produce print documents and 2-4 weeks to produce electronic documents. Shaun knew that production time could be shorter or longer based on the complexity of each customer's job.

3. Sales and Marketing

Shaun remembered a quote he learned in one of his business classes: "*People don't know what they want; they only want what they know.*" Shaun was aware that as a new startup company, he would need to invest a good deal of time and money to advertise and promote Decker's Digital Desktop. Shaun made a personal commitment to spend 8-10 hours every month to advertise and promote his business.

4. Accounting

Being the treasurer of his class and having taken several accounting courses, Shaun knew the importance of keeping accurate accounting records to manage his business. After seeking advice from his accounting teacher, Shaun realized that he could use a simple accounting system to manage the bookkeeping aspect of his business.

Shaun estimated it would take 1-2 hours per month to manage the accounting tasks associated with Decker's Digital Desktop.

5. Distribution

Shaun did not own his own car. Since Shaun's business required traveling to and from customers' sites, Shaun asked his parents if he could use the family car for business purposes.

Shaun's parents agreed to let him use the family car for business purposes under the following two conditions:

1. That they (Shaun's parents) accepted his business plan upon its completion
2. That Shaun pay a portion of the car insurance

Shaun agreed.

With the necessary background research completed, Shaun was ready to finish the "Operating Plan" section of his business plan.

> Shaun Decker's completed "Operating Plan" section of his business plan is provided on the next page.

Shaun Decker's Operating Plan:

Operating Plan

I. Purchasing

Materials required for product development:
- Various stocks of paper
- Printer toner

Suppliers of materials to be used in the direct production of products include:
- Quill Corporation (http://www.quill.com)
- Staples (http://www.staples.com)
- Computer Discount Warehouse (http://www.cdw.com)

These suppliers have been chosen for reasons of quality, price, and delivery turnaround. Materials ordered from these suppliers are generally received within 24–48 hours of order placement.

II. Production

Turnaround for products and services offered by Decker's Digital Desktop are as follows:
1. Print documents> 2–4 business days from order placement
2. Electronic documents> 2-4 weeks depending on the complexity of the job

III. Sales and Marketing

Because the business is a startup, during the initial few years, a minimum of 8-10 hours per month will be spent conducting marketing and promotional activities for Decker's Digital Desktop.

IV. Accounting

A simple automated accounting system will be maintained. It is estimated that accounting tasks for Decker's Digital Desktop will take 1-2 hours per month.

V. Distribution

Goods will be delivered to the customer's site using an automobile. Estimated delivery time per order is estimated at 30 minutes or less since all of Decker's Digital Desktop's customers will be located in the same community as the owner.

Now it's your turn to create the Operating Plan section of your business plan

Project 9:
Create the Operating Plan Section
of Your Business Plan

Follow the instructions provided below.

1. Using Microsoft Word, retrieve the file "Project9_Worksheet" from the "Teen Entrepreneur" folder installed from the Data CD.
2. Type your name and the current date in the header section of page 1 in the document.
3. Follow the instructions provided in the document to complete the worksheet.
4. Carefully proofread your work for accuracy and format.
5. Print a copy of the completed worksheet.
6. Save the completed worksheet to the "My Business Plan" folder.
7. Using Microsoft Word, open the file "Project9_Template" from the "Teen Entrepreneur" folder installed from the Data CD.
8. Complete all of the sections provided in the "Project9_Template" file to write the "Operating Plan" section of your business plan. Use the "Overview" notes and Shaun Decker's "Operating Plan" as a guide.
    Tip: Copy and paste the answers that are relevant from the "Project9_Worksheet" file.
9. Carefully proofread your work for accuracy and format.
10. Save the file as "Project9_Operating_Plan" to the "My Business Plan" folder.
11. Print a copy of the document.

Project 10:
Creating a Schedule of Startup Funds Required

Section of Your Business Plan

Approximate Completion Time: 1 hour

Business Plan Checklist

✓ Project 1: Choosing Your Teen-based Business
✓ Project 2: Company Description
✓ Project 3: Logo and Tagline
✓ Project 4: Description of Products and Services
✓ Project 5: Market Analysis
✓ Project 6: Business Card
✓ Project 7: Company Letterhead
✓ Project 8: Marketing Plan
✓ Project 9: Operating Plan
Project 10: Schedule of Startup Funds Required
Project 11: Customer Prospect Database
Project 12: Introductory Promotional Letter
Project 13: Three-Panel Brochure
Project 14: Newspaper Advertisement
Project 15: Owner's Resume
Project 16: Projected Income Statement
Project 17: Promotional Slide Show
Project 18: Executive Summary
Project 19: Business Plan Cover Page
Project 20: Final Assembly of Your Business Plan
Project 21: Company Web Site Homepage (*optional*)

INCLUDED IN THIS SECTION:

- Overview of the Schedule of Startup Funds Required
- See It In Action with Shaun Decker
- Now It's Your Turn to Build Your Business Plan

SOFTWARE REQUIRED:

 - Microsoft Excel

The Schedule of Startup Funds Required

THE TEEN ENTREPRENEUR

YOUR OBJECTIVE:

To produce the following section of your business plan:
• the Schedule of Startup Funds Required

BACKGROUND INFORMATION BEFORE YOU BEGIN:

What is a Schedule of Startup Funds Required and Why Have One?

A **Schedule of Startup Funds Required** is a financial statement which consists of an outline of all the equipment, supplies, and marketing expenses required to get a business up and running. It is important for every prospective new business owner to know exactly how much money will be required at startup. Many businesses that have high startup costs seek their startup funds from banks in the form of a "startup loan." Banks usually require that a Schedule of Startup Funds be included in the business plan.

To create a Schedule of Startup Funds Required, businesses usually use financial calculation software such as Microsoft Excel.

What's Included in a Schedule of Startup Funds Required?

A Schedule of Startup Funds Required includes the following items:

1. Cost of equipment required to start the business
2. Cost of materials and supplies required to start the business
3. Advertising and marketing costs required to start the business

Now let's learn how Shaun Decker created a Schedule of Startup Funds Required for his business plan

Shaun Decker's
Schedule of Startup Funds Required

Earlier in his business venture, you might recall that Shaun estimated he would need $5,000 to start his business. Shaun's parents have agreed to loan Shaun the startup money only if his business plan looks feasible. Using the data he gathered for his marketing and operating plans, Shaun had the necessary information to determine how much money he would need to start his desktop publishing business.

Shaun used Microsoft Excel to set up a "Schedule of Funds Required," which he would add to his business plan. Since Shaun already possessed a state-of-the-art computer system and all the required software necessary to run his business, these items would not have to be included in his Schedule of Startup Funds Required.

With the necessary background research complete, Shaun was ready to create the "Schedule of Startup Funds Required" section of his business plan.

> Shaun Decker's completed "Schedule of Startup Funds Required" section of his business plan is provided on the next page.

Shaun Decker's Schedule of Startup Funds Required:

Decker's Digital Desktop
Schedule of Startup Funds Required
Prepared by the owner, Shaun Decker

Startup funds available: **$5,000.00**

Equipment Required:	Price Ea.	Qty. Needed	Total
Laptop Computer	$1,500.00	1	$1,500.00
New Laser Printer	$400.00	1	$400.00
New Color Ink Jet Printer	$149.00	1	$149.00
Laser Toner	$79.00	2	$158.00
Color Ink Jet Cartridges	$29.00	4	$116.00
Digital Camera	$199.00	1	$199.00
Scanner	$149.00	1	$149.00

Materials and Supplies:			
Reams of Letterhead Paper	$15.99	4	$63.96
Packages of Business Card Stock	$19.99	4	$79.96
Packages of Brochure Paper	$24.99	4	$99.96
Reams of General Paper	$4.49	10	$44.90
Miscellaneous Office Supplies	$100.00	1	$100.00

Advertising:			
Newspaper Advertisement - 2 weeks	$100.00	2	$200.00
Direct mail to 200 businesses	$0.39	200	$78.00

Total Startup Funds Required: **$3,337.78**

Startup Funds Left Over: **$1,662.22**

Note: After analyzing his schedule of startup funds required, Shaun realized that he over-estimated the amount of startup money he would need to start his business. Being the businessman that he is, Shaun would still seek the full $5,000 loan from his parents and use the left-over startup money of $1,662.22 to grow his business.

Now it's your turn to create the Schedule of Startup Funds Required section of your business plan

Project 10:
Create the Schedule of Startup Funds Required Section for Your Business Plan

Follow the instructions provided below.

1. Using Microsoft Excel, retrieve the file "Project10_Template" from the "Teen Entrepreneur" folder installed from the Data CD.
2. Complete all of the sections labeled in the "Project10_Template" file to create the "Schedule of Startup Funds Required" section of your business plan. Use formulas to calculate totals where required. Use the "Overview" notes and Shaun Decker's "Schedule of Startup Funds Required" as a guide.

    Important Notes:

    • Depending on the type of business you have chosen, you may find it necessary to modify some of the contents in the "Project10_Template."

    • You may find it necessary to delete or add rows to the spreadsheet.
3. Carefully proofread your work for accuracy and format.
4. Save the file as "Project10_Startup_Funds" to the "My Business Plan" folder.
5. Print a copy of the document.

Project 11:
Creating a Customer
Prospect Database

For Your Business Plan

Approximate Completion Time: 2 hours

Business Plan Checklist

✓ Project 1:   Choosing Your Teen-based Business
✓ Project 2:   Company Description
✓ Project 3:   Logo and Tagline
✓ Project 4:   Description of Products and Services
✓ Project 5:   Market Analysis
✓ Project 6:   Business Card
✓ Project 7:   Company Letterhead
✓ Project 8:   Marketing Plan
✓ Project 9:   Operating Plan
✓ Project 10:   Schedule of Startup Funds Required
    Project 11:   Customer Prospect Database
    Project 12:   Introductory Promotional Letter
    Project 13:   Three-Panel Brochure
    Project 14:   Newspaper Advertisement
    Project 15:   Owner's Resume
    Project 16:   Projected Income Statement
    Project 17:   Promotional Slide Show
    Project 18:   Executive Summary
    Project 19:   Business Plan Cover Page
    Project 20:   Final Assembly of Your Business Plan
    Project 21:   Company Web Site Homepage (*optional*)

INCLUDED IN THIS SECTION:

- Overview of a Customer Prospect Database
- See It In Action with Shaun Decker
- Now It's Your Turn to Build Your Business Plan

SOFTWARE REQUIRED:

- Microsoft Access
- Adobe Acrobat Reader

The Customer Prospect Database

THE TEEN ENTREPRENEUR

YOUR OBJECTIVE:

To produce the following item to be included in your business plan:
• a Customer Prospect Database

BACKGROUND INFORMATION BEFORE YOU BEGIN:

What is a Database?

Companies use databases to store and organize important information relevant to their business. A **database** is a collection of records that contains a variety of information. A database is made up of *records*. A *record* is a collection of information about one unit in a database. For example, let's say a landscaping company uses a database to store and organize their customers' names, addresses, and telephone numbers. If the database contains a total of 200 customers, each individual customer would be considered one record in the database. Each record within a database is made up of *fields*. A *field* is a single element of information contained within a record. For example, a customer's name would be considered a field.

What is a Customer Prospect Database and Why Have One?

Just about every business uses a customer database. Customer databases allow businesses to keep track of who their customers are. The business can then use the information stored in the customer database to contact their customers, either by phone, mail, e-mail, or in person.

A customer prospect database is the same as a customer database except for one key difference. A **customer prospect database** is a collection of potential or prospective customers. In other words, the customers stored in a customer prospect database are not officially considered "customers" of the business; rather, they are customers who are identified as becoming potential customers. Using a customer prospect database allows businesses to generate more sales by turning "potential" customers into "active" customers.

What Does a Customer Prospect Database Consist of?

While databases in general can vary depending on the type of information needed for a particular business, a customer prospect database might include the following information (fields) about potential customers:

> Name
> Position/Title
> Organization/Company
> Address
> City
> State
> Zip Code
> Phone Number
> Fax Number
> E-mail Address
> Web Site Address

Where to Find Prospective Customers

Finding prospective customers sometimes requires hard work. A few good places to find prospective customers are:

- your local phone book.
- the Internet.
- your city or town's Chamber of Commerce.

Why Include a Customer Prospect Database in a Business Plan?

Including a database of prospective customers in a business plan demonstrates that the owner has taken the necessary steps to begin attracting new customers to the business.

Now let's learn how Shaun Decker created a Customer Prospect Database for his business plan

Shaun Decker's
Customer Prospect Database

Shaun realized that a majority of his marketing efforts, at least in the early stages of the business, would be through direct mailing and personal selling.

To ensure that he contact the right prospective customers, Shaun decided to create a customer prospect database for Decker's Digital Desktop. Shaun decided that his customer prospect database would be comprised of the following fields:

First Name	State
Last Name	Zip Code
Title	Phone Number
Company	Fax Number
Address	E-mail Address
City	Web Site Address

Shaun used the local telephone book and Chamber of Commerce Web site as his primary sources to gather information about potential customers. Shaun focused on creating a customer prospect database to include at least 20 small businesses that he identified as potentially needing desktop publishing services.

With this step complete, Shaun was ready to create his "Customer Prospect Database" for his business plan.

A portion of Shaun Decker's "Customer Prospect Database" is provided below.

Record #1

First Name	Damian
Last Name	Alberti
Title	Owner
Company	Pleasant Landing Vet
Address	111 Foxx Road
City	Pleasant Landing
State	NY
Zip	19999
Phone	315-999-2424
Fax	315-999-2434
E-mail	apdamian@plvet.com
Web	www.plvet.com

Record #2

First Name	Lucinda
Last Name	Chase
Title	Owner
Company	Chase Motel
Address	434 Central Blvd
City	Pleasant Landing
State	NY
Zip	19999
Phone	315-999-4444
Fax	315-999-4445
E-mail	lchase@chasemotel.com
Web	www.chasemotel.com

Record #3

First Name	Lance
Last Name	Evans
Title	Owner
Company	Edge Automotive
Address	1126 Central Blvd
City	Pleasant Landing
State	NY
Zip	19999
Phone	315-999-3343
Fax	315-999-4443
E-mail	levans@edgeauto.com
Web	www.edgeauto.com

Project 11: Customer Prospect Database

Record #4

First Name	Mark
Last Name	Falk
Title	Co-owner
Company	Falk Water Co.
Address	77 State Street
City	Pleasant Landing
State	NY
Zip	19999
Phone	315-999-8584
Fax	315-999-8883
E-mail	falkm@falkwater.com
Web	www.falkwater.com

Record #5

First Name	Beth
Last Name	Gregory
Title	Owner
Company	The Magik Garden
Address	820 East Main Street
City	Pleasant Landing
State	NY
Zip	19999
Phone	315-999-7766
Fax	315-999-7767
E-mail	owner@magikgarden.com
Web	www.magikgarden.com

Record #6

First Name	Michael
Last Name	Lawrence
Title	Co-owner
Company	Land-Locked Contractors
Address	88 Birch Drive
City	Pleasant Landing
State	NY
Zip	19999
Phone	315-999-6464
Fax	315-999-6565
E-mail	Michaell@land-locked.com
Web	www.land-locked.com

Record #7

First Name	Giorgio
Last Name	Marolla
Title	Owner
Company	Mama Giorgio's Italian Villa
Address	411 Granite Street
City	Pleasant Landing
State	NY
Zip	19999
Phone	315-999-1234
Fax	315-999-4321
E-mail	mama@giorgios.com
Web	www.giorgios.com

Record #8

First Name	Katherine
Last Name	Martin
Title	Owner
Company	Martin's Hair Salon
Address	17 State Street
City	Pleasant Landing
State	NY
Zip	19999
Phone	315-999-8908
Fax	N/A
E-mail	N/A
Web	N/A

Record #9

First Name	Eugene
Last Name	Samuels
Title	Owner
Company	Lettuce Do Lunch
Address	312 Main Ave
City	Pleasant Landing
State	NY
Zip	19999
Phone	315-999-5878
Fax	315-999-7849
E-mail	eugenes@dolunch.com
Web	www.dolunch.com

Now it's your turn to create a
Customer Prospect Database
for your business plan

Project 11:
Create a Customer Prospect
Database for Your Business Plan

Follow the instructions provided below.

1. Open the file "Project11_Database_Planning_Form" from the "Teen Entrepreneur" folder installed from the Data CD. Print a copy of the document and follow the instructions provided. ***Note:*** *You will need Adobe Acrobat Reader to view and print this document.*

2. Using Microsoft Access, create a new database.

3. Name the new database "Project11_Database" and store it in the "My Business Plan" folder.

4. Create a new table within the database and name the table "Customer Prospect Database."

5. Define the following fields in the database: (*Use the "Overview" notes and Shaun Decker's "Customer Prospect Database" as a guide.*)

First Name	State
Last Name	Zip
Title	Phone
Company	Fax
Address	E-mail
City	Web

6. Using the information you collected on the "Customer Prospect Database Planning Form," enter each customer prospect record in the database. ***Note:*** *You must include a minimum of 10 records in your database.*

7. Carefully proofread your work for accuracy and format.

8. Print a copy of the database.

    Keep the document in a secure place as you will need to add it to your Business Plan at the conclusion of this simulation.

Project 12:
Creating an Introductory Promotional Letter

For Your Business Plan

Approximate Completion Time: 1.5 hours

Business Plan Checklist

INCLUDED IN THIS SECTION:

- Overview of an Introductory Promotional Letter
- See It In Action with Shaun Decker
- Now It's Your Turn to Build Your Business Plan

SOFTWARE REQUIRED:

- Microsoft Word
- Microsoft Access

The Introductory Promotional Letter

THE TEEN ENTREPRENEUR

YOUR OBJECTIVE:

To produce the following item to be included in your business plan:
- an Introductory Promotional Letter

BACKGROUND INFORMATION BEFORE YOU BEGIN:

What is an Introductory Promotional Letter and Why Use One?

An **introductory promotional letter** is a business letter written with the intent of introducing a new business to prospective customers while at the same time providing the recipient with a call to action in the form of a *premium*.

A *premium* is a promotional tool that serves to elicit a response from a potential customer. Some examples of premiums include:
- "Buy-One-Get-One-Free" offers
- Introductory discounts
- Free delivery
- Free gift with first order
- Coupons

Why Include an Introductory Promotional Letter in a Business Plan?

Including a promotional letter demonstrates that the owner has taken the initiative to begin promoting, advertising, and attracting new customers to the business.

If included, a promotional letter is usually put as a supplemental attachment or in the appendix in a business plan.

> **Now let's learn how Shaun Decker created an Introductory Promotional Letter for his business plan**

Shaun Decker's
Introductory Promotional Letter

Shaun decided to use direct mail to introduce himself and Decker's Digital Desktop to prospective customers. His mail piece would consist of a letter that would introduce Decker's Digital Desktop to prospective new customers. The contents of the letter would be placed on the company letterhead Shaun previously created. As Shaun began writing the letter using Microsoft Word, he brainstormed several possible promotions that would attract new customers. After narrowing down the ideas, Shaun decided to include the following *premium* offer in the letter:

"Purchase 500 business cards and get an additional 100 free."

With the letter complete, Shaun used the mail merge feature in Microsoft Word to merge the letter with his customer prospect database to complete this project. Shaun decided to include his introductory promotional letter as a supplemental attachment in his business plan.

> Shaun Decker's "Introductory Promotional Letter" is provided on the next page.

Shaun Decker's Introductory Promotional Letter:

DECKER'S DIGITAL DESKTOP
The Image of Your Future

Shaun Decker, Owner
123 Prescott Ave • Pleasant Landing, NY 19999
Phone: (315) 999-9797 • www.DeckersDigitalDesktop.com

Desktop Publishing • Web Development

September 1, 2006

<<First Name>> <<Last Name>>, <<Title>>
<<Company>>
<<Address>>
<<City>>, <<State>> <<Zip>>

Mail merge fields from Shaun's Customer Prospect Database

Dear <<First Name>>,

I would like to take this opportunity to introduce Decker's Digital Desktop.

Decker's Digital Desktop was founded in 2006 for the purpose of providing businesses in the Pleasant Landing community with a one-stop source for all their publishing needs. We pride ourselves on the individualized service we are able to provide for our customers from order placement through final delivery. Our printed products are produced using the finest quality paper stock available on the market. Check out our Web page design and development services at www.DeckersDigitalDesktop.com.

Take advantage of our introductory offer!
Place an order for a minimum of 500 business cards, and get an additional
100 cards absolutely FREE!

Let us show you what Decker's Digital Desktop can do for your business image.

Very truly yours,

Shaun Decker
Owner

Now it's your turn to create your
**Introductory Promotional Letter and merge
it with your Customer Prospect Database**

Project 12:
Create an Introductory Promotional Letter for Your Business Plan

Follow the instructions provided below.

1. Using Microsoft Word, open the file "Project7_Letterhead" (your company's letterhead) from the "My Business Plan" folder. Save this file as "Project12_Promo_Letter" to the "My Business Plan" folder.

2. Add the current date, body, and closing of your introductory promotional letter to the document. Be sure to include an introductory premium in your letter. Use the "Overview" notes and Shaun Decker's "Introductory Promotional Letter" as a guide.

3. Perform a mail merge with the "Customer Prospect Database" you created in Project 11 as follows:

    a. From the *Tools* menu choose *Mail Merge.*

    b. For the *Main Document*, choose *Create>Form Letters>Active Window.*

    c. For the *Data Source*, choose *Get Data>Open Data Source.* Open the Microsoft Access database file "Project11_Database" from the "My Business Plan" folder. Choose the table titled "Customer Prospect Database."

    d. Insert the following Merge Fields in the appropriate places in the letter: (*Use Shaun Decker's "Introductory Promotional Letter" as a visual guide.*)
        First Name, Last Name, Title, Company, Address, City, State, Zip

    e. Merge the document.

    f. Save the merged document as "Project12_Merged" to the "My Business Plan" folder.

4. Carefully proofread your work for accuracy and format.

5. Print a copy of **ONE** letter from the merged file.

    Keep the document in a secure place as you will need to add it to your Business Plan at the conclusion of this simulation.

Courtesy of Junior Achievement.

Nicole Knothe of Eden Prairie, MN
Company: Swim Instructor

Nicole Knothe is an extremely passionate young lady, and her business is a shining example of her caring and selfless attitude. Nicole runs a swim teaching program, which helps kids from kindergarten to high school with all aspects of their swimming skill-sets.

Nicole offers lessons to all types of children—those that are scared at the sight of water to someone who loves the water, and just needs help on stroke technique.

"The reason my business is different than other swim programs is because it's more personal," claims Nicole. "I grow to be more of a friend with the children and their families than just someone who teaches swim lessons."

As Nicole has recently embarked on her college career, she has put her business on hold. She does, however, plan to pick things back up during the summer months.

Project 13:
Creating a
Three-Panel Brochure

For Your Business Plan

Approximate Completion Time: 2–3 hours

Business Plan Checklist

INCLUDED IN THIS SECTION:

- Overview of a Three-Panel Brochure
- See It In Action with Shaun Decker
- Now It's Your Turn to Build Your Business Plan

SOFTWARE REQUIRED:

- Microsoft Publisher or Any Desktop Publishing Software
- Adobe Acrobat Reader

The Three-Panel Brochure

THE TEEN ENTREPRENEUR

YOUR OBJECTIVE:

To produce the following item to be included in your business plan:
 • a Three-Panel Brochure

BACKGROUND INFORMATION BEFORE YOU BEGIN:

What is a Brochure and Why Have One?

A **brochure** is a small booklet or pamphlet, often containing promotional material and product information. Brochures are usually folded into two, three, or four panels. Brochures are popular because they are relatively small when folded and take up less desk or file space for the recipient. Brochures are also relatively inexpensive to produce, making them a staple document for most businesses.

A brochure can serve several purposes. It can inform people about your business and its history. Brochures educate customers about the products and/or services a business offers. They can serve as sales tools used to persuade a potential customer to purchase from your business. A brochure should entice the reader to want to further explore doing business with you.

What to Include in a Brochure

A well-designed brochure usually includes the following information about a business:

1. Name of the business
2. Mailing address
3. Telephone and fax numbers
4. Web site address
5. Logo and tagline
6. Contact person's name and job title from the business
7. E-mail address
8. Graphic images to help illustrate what your business provides to the customer
9. List of products and/or services offered
10. Prices of products and/or services offered
11. A brief company history
12. Key benefits of the business
13. A call to action (something to entice the reader to inquire further)

Three-Panel Brochure Design Tips and Guidelines

To project a professional image, the layout and design of your brochure should be consistent with that of your business card and letterhead.

When designing a three-panel brochure, consider the following design tips and guidelines:

1. **Do Not Overcrowd.** Do not clutter the elements included on each panel in the brochure. Leave plenty of "white" space to make each area easy to read and pleasing to the eye.
2. **Minimize Typefaces (Fonts).** Use no more than two or three different typefaces (fonts) in your brochure. This helps to create a clean, crisp, professional look.
3. **Keep Elements in Proportion.** Keep the size and proportion of each element on the brochure balanced and symmetrical.
4. **Minimize Color.** If you will be printing your brochure using a color printer, keep the number of colors to a minimum. Remember to keep your color scheme consistent with those used in your logo and/or on your business card and letterhead.
5. **Use Short blocks of Text.** Keep the amount of text you place in one particular area to a minimum. This helps to keep the reader moving through the brochure and from getting "bored."
6. **Use Headings and Subheadings.** Divide chunks of information by using bold headings and/or subheadings in the brochure.

Why Include a Brochure in a Business Plan?

Including a brochure in a business plan provides the reader with a visual "snapshot" of the business. A brochure helps project a professional image and identity to the reader.

Understanding the Page Setup of a Three-Panel Brochure

A three-panel brochure is a document consisting of one sheet of paper with print on both sides. This is known as a two-sided document. The brochure is folded equally into thirds, which makes up the three panels for each side. The graphic shown in Figure 13.1 illustrates both sides of a three-panel brochure.

Figure 13.1: Illustration of a Three-Panel Brochure

Side 1: Outside of brochure

| Outside left panel | Outside middle panel | Outside right panel |

Fold   Fold

Side 2: Inside of brochure

| Inside left panel | Inside middle panel | Inside right panel |

Fold   Fold

Fold   Fold

Outside right panel   Inside right panel

When folded, the brochure should look like this

Now let's look at the Three-Panel Brochure Shaun Decker created for his business plan

Shaun Decker's
Three-Panel Brochure

As another form of advertising and promoting his business, Shaun decided to create a three-panel brochure. Following his marketing plan, Shaun would either hand deliver the brochures to local businesses or send them by direct mail.

Shaun sat down and began experimenting with several different layout and design possibilities for his three-panel brochure. He wanted to create a brochure that was consistent with the design and style of his business card and company letterhead. After several layout changes and text rewrites, Shaun believed he had developed the perfect brochure for his business. He planned to add the brochure as a supplemental attachment to his business plan.

> Both sides of Shaun Decker's completed "Three-Panel Brochure" are provided on the next page.

Side 1 of Shaun Decker's Three-Panel Brochure:

All About Us

Decker's Digital Desktop was founded in 2006 for the purpose of providing Pleasant Landing area businesses with a one-stop source for all their printing needs.

We pride ourselves on providing individualized custom printing and design services.

We meet with our customers onsite so we can cater our printing and design services to your business.

Our printed products are produced using the finest quality paper stock available on the market.

Whether you need business cards or an elaborate Web presence, Decker's Digital Desktop has all the tools to achieve the business image you desire.

Specializing in fine quality print and electronic documents

Shaun Decker, Owner
123 Prescott Ave • Pleasant Landing, NY 19999
Phone: (315) 999-9797
www.DeckersDigitalDesktop.com

Desktop Publishing • Web Development

www.DeckersDigitalDesktop.com

Side 2 of Shaun Decker's Three-Panel Brochure:

Print Documents

Business Cards
Letterhead
Brochures

Word Processing Services

Reports
Resumes
Books
Catalogs
And more!

Electronic Documents

Presentation Development
Web Site Development

Free Delivery!

INTRODUCTORY OFFER

FREE 100 BUSINESS CARDS

with your first order of 500 business cards

Limited one-time offer per customer

Shaun Decker, Owner
123 Prescott Ave • Pleasant Landing, NY 19999
Phone: (315) 999-9797
www.DeckersDigitalDesktop.com

Pricing

Business Cards (priced per 500 cards)	$75.00
Brochures (priced per 200 brochures)	$105.00
Letterhead (priced per 500 sheets)	$85.00
Web Site Development	$50.00/hr.
Presentation Development	$30.00/hr.
Word Processing	$4.50/pg.

For specialty jobs, please call for a free estimate.

Now it's your turn to create a Three-Panel Brochure for your business plan

Project 13:
Create a Three-Panel Brochure
for Your Business Plan

Follow the instructions provided below.

1. Open the file "Project13_Brochure_Planning_Form" from the "Teen Entrepreneur" folder installed from the Data CD. Print a copy of the document and follow the instructions provided. ***Note:*** *You will need Adobe Acrobat Reader to view and print this document.*

2. Using Microsoft Publisher (or any desktop publishing software), create a new document.

3. Set up your document according to the page setup instructions provided on the next page. → **Go to next page**

4. Place the contents of both sides of your brochure in the appropriate panels. Use the "Overview" notes and Shaun Decker's "Three-Panel Brochure" as a guide.

5. Carefully proofread your work for accuracy and format.

6. Save the file as "Project13_Brochure" to the "My Business Plan" folder.

7. Print both sides of your brochure.

   Keep the brochure in a secure place as you will need to add it to your Business Plan at the conclusion of this simulation.

Page setup instructions for the three-panel brochure:

1. Set the page dimensions to 11 inches wide x 8.5 inches tall.
2. Set the page orientation to landscape (wide).
3. Set the number of pages to 2.
4. Set the page margins to .25 inches on all sides.
5. Use page or column guides to divide both pages (both sides of the brochure) into three equal panels. Leave a .5 inch gutter space between each column to allow for folding. Do not place any contents inside the .5 inch gutter spaces on either side of the brochure. *Refer to the illustration provided below for more assistance.*

Page 1 (Side 1): Outside of brochure

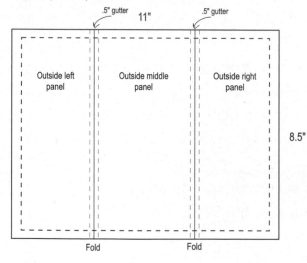

Page 2 (Side 2): Inside of brochure

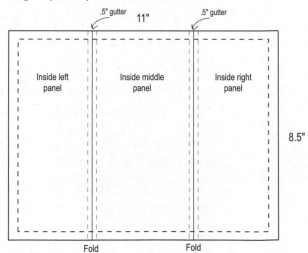

Project 14:
Creating a Newspaper Advertisement

For Your Business Plan

Approximate Completion Time: 1 hour

Business Plan Checklist

INCLUDED IN THIS SECTION:

- Overview of a Newspaper Advertisement
- See It In Action with Shaun Decker
- Now It's Your Turn to Build Your Business Plan

SOFTWARE REQUIRED:

- Microsoft Word, Microsoft Publisher, or Any Desktop Publishing Software
- Adobe Acrobat Reader

The Newspaper Advertisement

THE TEEN ENTREPRENEUR

YOUR OBJECTIVE:

To produce the following item to be included in your business plan:
- a Newspaper Advertisement

BACKGROUND INFORMATION BEFORE YOU BEGIN:

Why Use a Newspaper Advertisement?

Newspapers are the world's most widely read type of periodicals. Newspaper businesses earn their money in two ways:

1. By paid subscribers
2. By paid advertisers

Many businesses use regional, state, and/or local newspapers to reach their target audiences. Advertisers have a choice as to how large their advertisement appears in a newspaper. The larger the advertisement, the higher the price they will pay. Businesses also can choose where an advertisement appears in a newspaper. A Wedding Disc Jockey business, for example, can choose to have its advertisement placed in the Wedding section.

What Should a Newspaper Advertisement Include?

An advertisement in a newspaper or other periodicals should:

1. be designed to immediately grab the attention of the reader.
2. be easy to read and understand.
3. contain a call to action.
4. include the company name, address, and other contact information.
5. include a company logo and tagline.

Why Include an Advertisement in a Business Plan?

Including an advertisement in a business plan accomplishes the following:

1. It shows the owner's ability to create and design an effective marketing piece.
2. It shows the reader the owner is "speaking" to potential customers.
3. It demonstrates the owner's ability to reach the target audience.

If included, an advertisement is usually put as a supplemental attachment or in the appendix of a business plan.

Now let's look at the Newspaper Advertisement Shaun Decker created for his business plan

Shaun Decker's Newspaper Advertisement

Following his marketing paln, Shaun's next step was to create an advertisement that would run in his local newspaper, *The Pleasant Landing Times*. Shaun would reserve advertising space to run the ad during his first month in business. Based on Shaun's previous research, he could afford to run a 5 inch wide by 7 inch tall ad.

The goal of Shaun's ad is to capture the attention of his audience again by using the "free business card" promotion he used in his brochure. Using his brochure as the basis for his design and layout, Shaun sat down to begin creating the newspaper advertisement.

Shaun would add his newspaper advertisement as a supplmental attachment to his business plan.

Shaun Decker's completed "Newspaper Advertisement" is provided on the next page.

Shaun Decker's Newspaper Advertisement:

Now it's your turn to create a Newspaper Advertisement for your business plan

Project 14:
Create a Newspaper Advertisement for Your Business Plan

Follow the instructions provided below.

1. Open the file "Project14_Ad_Planning_Form" from the "Teen Entrepreneur" folder installed from the Data CD. Print a copy of the document and follow the instructions provided. **Note:** You will need Adobe Acrobat Reader to view and print this document.
2. Using Microsoft Word, Microsoft Publisher (or any desktop publishing software), create a new document.
3. Draw a bordered frame measuring 5 inches wide by 7 inches tall. Place this frame in the center of your document.
4. Place the contents of your newspaper advertisement inside the bordered frame. Use the "Overview" notes and Shaun Decker's "Newspaper Advertisement" as a guide.
5. Carefully proofread your work for accuracy and format.
6. Save the file as "Project14_Advertisement" to the "My Business Plan" folder.
7. Print a copy of the document.

   Keep the document in a secure place as you will need to add it to your Business Plan at the conclusion of this simulation.

Real Teen Entrepreneur Success Story

Courtesy of Junior Achievement.

Seth Flowerman of Morristown, NJ
Company: Career Explorations LLC

Seth Flowerman is president of Career Explorations LLC, which organizes and runs a residential summer internship program for high school students from around the country.

Participants live at The Juilliard School in the heart of New York City, intern for top organizations during the day, and attend group activities such as concerts in Central Park, sporting events, and Broadway musicals in the evenings. A "getting to know New York" scavenger hunt, a Career Night with top business executives, college visits, and a group community service project round out the program. More information about Career Explorations is available online at *www.ceinternships.com*.

"I am honored that the panel from the Young Entrepreneurs' Organization and the World Entrepreneurs' Organization selected me as the Entrepreneur of the Year," said Seth.

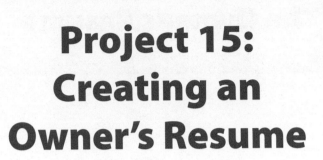

Project 15: Creating an Owner's Resume

For Your Business Plan

Approximate Completion Time: 1 hour

INCLUDED IN THIS SECTION:

- Overview of the Owner's Resume
- See It In Action with Shaun Decker
- Now It's Your Turn to Build Your Business Plan

SOFTWARE REQUIRED:

- Microsoft Word
- Adobe Acrobat Reader

Business Plan Checklist

The Owner's Resume

THE TEEN ENTREPRENEUR

YOUR OBJECTIVE:

To produce the following item to be included in your business plan:
- an Owner's Resume

BACKGROUND INFORMATION BEFORE YOU BEGIN:

What is a Resume and Why Have One?

A **resume** is a brief autobiographical sketch containing information important to a prospective employer, potential business investor, or prospective customer of your business.

Information contained in the resume includes work experience, educational background, related skills, and other qualifications. Resumes are usually not more than one to two pages in length.

Types of Resumes

A resume can be formatted in a variety of ways depending on the purpose for which it is being used.

The following is a list and brief description of some of the most common types of resumes.

1. **The Chronological Resume.** The Chronological Resume lists work experience first and in reverse chronological order (most recent employment first), with educational background and skills listed as secondary. This format is best used by individuals who have a considerable amount of work experience to list on the resume.

2. **The Functional Resume.** The Functional Resume puts primary importance on skills, with work experience and education listed as secondary. This format is best for individuals who have considerable work skills that would be of greater interest to the reader than educational or experiential qualifications.

3. **The Combination Resume.** The Combination Resume focuses equally on all components included within a resume. This format is best used by individuals who have strong educational qualifications, considerable work experience, and other information (versatile set of skills, considerable community service, etc.) of equal importance.

Resume Tips and Guidelines

First impressions count! As a result, choose a resume format that is most suitable to your individual circumstances.

When composing a resume, consider that it must:
1. sell the reader in the top half.
2. be tailored to the audience.
3. contain only brief descriptive statements (lengthy paragraphs should be avoided).
4. be eye-appealing. The resume should contain balanced margins and spacing, contain a consistent style and color, and important components should be highlighted in bold print.
5. contain no grammatical or spelling errors.
6. remain a single page in length, if at all possible (front and back are acceptable).

When composing the resume, you should not:
1. list hobbies unless they relate to the position for which you are applying.
2. list references. References should be listed on a separate references page that is given out only upon request.
3. list salary requirements or past salaries.
4. give reasons for leaving previous employers.
5. list personal information such as age, sex, weight, height, and marital status.
6. include a photo or incorporate a digital image of yourself into the document.

Why Include an Owner's Resume in a Business Plan?

Adding an owner's resume allows readers of a business plan to assess the owner's abilities to run and operate the business. By looking at the owner's educational background, work experience, and personal skills and abilities, potential investors of the business can conduct a "paper" interview through the resume.

Now let's look at the Resume Shaun Decker created for his business plan

Shaun Decker's Resume

To develop his personal resume, Shaun Decker sat down and wrote an outline of his education, work experience, certificates, and extracurricular activities. Although most resumes include a "job objective" statement, Shaun did not include one on his resume since he was not applying for a job. After a great deal of thought and a few rewrites, Shaun believed he had a solid, well-written resume to add to his business plan.

Shaun Decker's completed "Resume" is provided on the next page.

Shaun Decker's Resume:

123 PRESCOTT AVENUE · PLEASANT LANDING, NY 19999 · 315.999-9797

SHAUN DECKER

EDUCATION

2002-Present   Pleasant Landing High School · Pleasant Landing, NY
Major in Business

WORK EXPERIENCE

2006-Present   Decker's Digital Desktop · Pleasant Landing, NY
Owner
New startup desktop publishing business

2003-2005   Valley Audio, Video, & Computers · Pleasant Landing, NY
Clerk/Salesperson
Responsible for customer service, checkout, stocking shelves

2002-2006   Decker's Lawn Care · Pleasant Landing, NY
Owner
Responsible for all business operations

ACHIEVEMENTS

· Certified Microsoft Office Specialist (Word, Excel, PowerPoint)
· Currently preparing for Microsoft Office Specialist exam in Access
· Named 2005 Business Student of the Year (Pleasant Landing High School)

EXTRACURRICULAR ACTIVITIES

2004-Present   FBLA President, Pleasant Landing High School
2003-Present   Treasurer, Pleasant Landing High School Class of 2006
2003-Present   Varsity Soccer
2003-Present   Varsity Hockey
2003-Present   Drummer, Pleasant Landing High School Senior Band
2003-Present   Member: Academy of Finance

REFERENCES

Available upon request

Now it's your turn to create a Resume
for your business plan

Project 15:
Create an Owner's Resume
for Your Business Plan

Follow the instructions provided below.

1. Open the file "Project15_Resume_Planning_Form" from the "Teen Entrepreneur" folder installed from the Data CD. Print a copy of the document and follow the instructions provided. *Note: You will need Adobe Acrobat Reader to view and print this document.*

2. Using Microsoft Word, create a new document.

3. Using the information you added to the "Resume Planning Form," create an owner's resume for your business plan. Use the "Overview" notes and Shaun Decker's "Resume" as a guide to assist you in the format and design of your resume.

4. Carefully proofread your work for accuracy and format.

5. Save the file as "Project15_Resume" to the "My Business Plan" folder.

6. Print a copy of the document.

Project 16:
Creating a Projected Income Statement

For Your Business Plan

Approximate Completion Time: 1 hour

MY BUSINESS PLAN

INCLUDED IN THIS SECTION:

- Overview of the Projected Income Statement
- See It In Action with Shaun Decker
- Now It's Your Turn to Build Your Business Plan

SOFTWARE REQUIRED:

- Microsoft Excel
- Adobe Acrobat Reader

Business Plan Checklist

The Projected Income Statement

THE TEEN ENTREPRENEUR

YOUR OBJECTIVE:

To produce the following section of your business plan:
• a Projected Income Statement

BACKGROUND INFORMATION BEFORE YOU BEGIN:

What is an Income Statement?

An **Income Statement** is a financial report that businesses use to summarize revenues (sales) and expenses—showing the net profit or loss in a specified accounting period (month, quarter, year). Income Statements are also called "profit and loss statements" or "statement of revenue and expenses." In short, the Income Statement provides a snapshot of a business's performance over time.

Components of an Income Statement

There are five basic components that are included in an Income Statement:

1. **Net Sales**
   Net Sales include the sales of goods or services (called revenue) during a specified accounting period less the cost of any returns or allowances. *Returns* are items that were originally sold to the customer but returned. *Allowances* are reductions in the normal sales price due to item defects, rebates offered, discounts, etc.

2. **Cost of Goods Sold**
   Cost of Goods Sold (COGS) includes any expenses directly related to the production or the purchase of items for sale during a specified accounting period.

3. **Gross Profit**
   Gross Profit is the amount of money remaining once the cost of goods sold is deducted from Net Sales (revenue).
   • Gross Profit shown as a formula is: *Gross Profit = Net Sales – COGS*

4. **Operating Expenses**
   Operating Expenses include any expenses directly related to running the day-to-day operations of the business.

5. **Net Income**
   Net Income is the amount of money remaining once the Total Operating Expenses are deducted from the Gross Profit. If the Net Income is a positive number, the business incurs a profit. If the Net Income is a negative number, the business incurs a loss.
   • Net Income shown as a formula is: *Net Income = Gross Profit – Operating Expenses*

What is a Projected Income Statement and Why Include One in a Business Plan?

It is important for a new business to forecast or make educated projections as to what its financial future will look like. A **Projected Income Statement** is identical to an Income Statement, with the exception of one thing: a Projected Income Statement includes estimated figures rather than actual ones.

Projected Income Statements are a way for new businesses to look into a "crystal ball" to see what kind of profit or loss can be expected for a specified accounting period. This is why they are usually included in the business plan.

It should be noted that it is important for the estimated figures used in a Projected Income Statement to be calculated using researched data and figures. Otherwise, the Projected Income Statement might become embellished providing the business with a false projection of Net Income.

Now let's learn how Shaun Decker created a Projected Income Statement for his business plan

Shaun Decker's Projected Income Statement

Shaun was excited to put together a projected income statement for his new desktop publishing business. After all, he knew that if he included accurate figures based on his previous research, the Projected Income Statement would hold the answer to Shaun's bottom-line potential profits. What follows is an overview of how Shaun developed the information necessary to create his "Projected Income Statement" for his business plan.

Shaun's Specified Accounting Period

Shaun decided to create his Projected Income Statement by forecasting his first year in business.

Other Figures Needed to Complete Shaun's Projected Income Statement

From his previous research, Shaun already had all the data to include for the revenue and cost of goods sold sections of his projected income statement.

For the operating expenses section, however, Shaun needed to do some more research. Shaun had already researched his advertising, startup, and office supplies expenses. His research yielded that the following operating expenses would also be required to operate Decker's Digital Desktop:

> • **Phone Expense.** Shaun would use his parents' phone to conduct business out of the home. Shaun's parents agreed that since Shaun would be using their phone to conduct business, he should pay a percentage of the monthly phone bill. It was decided that Shaun would pay $10 per month for the use of the phone.

> • **Auto Insurance Expense.** Since Shaun would be using his parents' car to meet with customers and deliver their products, Shaun's parents agreed that he should be responsible for paying a portion of the auto insurance. His parents decided to charge Shaun $20 per month for car insurance.

• **Gas Expense.** Shaun's parents agreed to charge Shaun $20 per month for gas to use their car to conduct business.

• **Bank Fees.** The last operating expense Shaun would need to operate Decker's Digital Desktop was a checking account. A checking account would allow Shaun to keep accurate accounting records, pay vendors for supplies and materials, and make deposits. The monthly maintenance fee to maintain a checking account was $10.

Shaun's Projected Income Statement

Having all the necessary figures, Shaun sat down at his computer and used Microsoft Excel to create a Projected Income Statement for his first year in business.

Shaun Decker's completed "Projected Income Statement" is provided on the next page.

Shaun Decker's Projected Income Statement:

Decker's Digital Desktop
Projected Income Statement - Year 1
Prepared by the owner, Shaun Decker

REVENUE:

Sales:	Customers	Price	Totals
Business Cards	45	$75.00	$3,375.00
Brochures	25	$105.00	$2,625.00
Letterhead	30	$85.00	$2,550.00
Web Site Development	15	$200.00	$3,000.00
(Avg. 4 hrs. per customer $50/hr.=$200 per customer)			
Presentation Development	10	$150.00	$1,500.00
(Avg. 3 hrs. per customer $50/hr.=$150 per customer)			
Word Processing	40	$13.50	$540.00
(Avg. 3 pgs. per customer $4.50/pg.=$13.50 per customer)			
Other	10	$50.00	$500.00
Total Sales:			**$14,090.00**
Less Returns and Allowances			$0.00
Total Net Sales:			**$14,090.00**

LESS COST OF GOODS SOLD:

Item	Estimate Qty.	Price Ea.	Totals
Business Card Stock (per pkg. of 1,000)	20	$19.99	$399.80
Letterhead Stock Paper (per ream of 1,000)	15	$15.99	$239.85
Brochure Stock Paper (per pkg.)	10	$24.99	$249.90
Total Cost of Goods Sold:			**$889.55**

Gross Profit:			**$13,200.45**

OPERATING EXPENSES:

Item	Totals
Startup Expenses	$3,337.78
Ink Jet Cartridge	$116.00
Laser Toner	$79.00
Advertising	$400.00
Telephone ($10 per month)	$120.00
Auto Insurance ($20 per month)	$240.00
Gas ($20 per month)	$240.00
Bank Fees ($10 per month)	$120.00
Office Supplies	$250.00
Total Operating Expenses:	**$4,902.78**

Net Income:	**$8,297.67**

Now it's your turn to create a Projected Income Statement for your business plan

Project 16:
Create a Projected Income Statement for Your Business Plan

Follow the instructions provided below.

1. Open the file "Project16_Income_Statement_Worksheet" from the "Teen Entrepreneur" folder installed from the Data CD. Print a copy of the document and follow the instructions provided. ***Note:*** *You will need Adobe Acrobat Reader to view and print this document.*

2. Using Microsoft Excel, create a new workbook.

3. Using the information you added to the "Projected First Year Income Statement Worksheet," create a "Projected Income Statement" for your business plan. Use the "Overview" notes and Shaun Decker's "Projected Income Statement" as a guide.

4. Carefully proofread your work for accuracy and format.

5. Save the file as "Project16_Income_Statement" to the "My Business Plan" folder.

6. Print a copy of the document.

Courtesy of Junior Achievement.

Shreyans Parekh of Cerritos, CA
Company: Koyal Wholesale

Shreyans Parekh is an 18-year-old freshman at the University of Pennsylvania's Huntsman Program, pursuing a joint degree in business and international studies.

In January 2003, he began his career as an entrepreneur, co-founding a wholesale party and wedding supply company, Koyal Wholesale (*www.koyal.com*). Beginning as an online provider of balloons, party goods, novelty items, and favors at wholesale prices, Shreyans sent out orders from his home as he received them. With the swift success of his business, he quickly expanded, leasing a 10,000-square-foot warehouse to run his operation.

Shreyans recently hired five employees, and in a span of two years, has built one of the largest wholesale distributors of balloons, flags, and wedding supplies in the Inland Empire.

As the founder and marketing director of the company, Shreyans has performed many acts of philanthropy for his community. He is the co-founder of the humanitarian rights organization *See Evil, End Evil (SEEDE)*, which is currently working on a project to help build the first public library in Rwanda.

Project 17: Creating a Promotional Slide Show

For Your Business Plan

Approximate Completion Time: 1-2 hours

INCLUDED IN THIS SECTION:

- Overview of a Promotional Slide Show
- See It In Action with Shaun Decker
- Now It's Your Turn to Build Your Business Plan

SOFTWARE REQUIRED:

- Microsoft Word
- Microsoft PowerPoint
- Adobe Acrobat Reader

Business Plan Checklist

✓ Project 1:   Choosing Your Teen-based Business
✓ Project 2:   Company Description
✓ Project 3:   Logo and Tagline
✓ Project 4:   Description of Products and Services
✓ Project 5:   Market Analysis
✓ Project 6:   Business Card
✓ Project 7:   Company Letterhead
✓ Project 8:   Marketing Plan
✓ Project 9:   Operating Plan
✓ Project 10: Schedule of Startup Funds Required
✓ Project 11: Customer Prospect Database
✓ Project 12: Introductory Promotional Letter
✓ Project 13: Three-Panel Brochure
✓ Project 14: Newspaper Advertisement
✓ Project 15: Owner's Resume
✓ Project 16: Projected Income Statement
  Project 17: Promotional Slide Show
  Project 18: Executive Summary
  Project 19: Business Plan Cover Page
  Project 20: Final Assembly of Your Business Plan
  Project 21: Company Web Site Homepage (*optional*)

Promotional Slide Show

THE TEEN ENTREPRENEUR

YOUR OBJECTIVE:

To produce the following item to be included in your business plan:
   • a Promotional Slide Show

BACKGROUND INFORMATION BEFORE YOU BEGIN:

What is a Promotional Slide Show and Why Have One?

A **promotional slide show** is created using a presentation software program such as Microsoft PowerPoint. Slide shows are an effective promotional tool in that they give the audience a visual screen to look at, as opposed to a paper document.

Promotional slide shows can serve a variety of purposes including:
   1. To educate potential customers about the business
   2. To advertise products and/or services
   3. To advertise a special promotion offered by the business

A slide show is a versatile promotional tool that can easily be set up to run on desktop and laptop computers, large-screen monitors, slide screens, or televisions. Slide shows can be used at trade shows, malls, customer sites, and inside the premises of a business itself.

Things to Know Before Creating a Slide Show

Before creating a slide show, it is important to:

1. Identify the Purpose
You should be able to answer the following question:
   • *Is the purpose of the slide show to inform the audience, persuade the audience, or entertain the audience?*

2. Identify the Audience

You should be able to answer the following questions:

- *How many people will be in the audience?*
- *What is the age range of the audience?*
- *What is the educational level of the audience? Does the audience have any familiarity with the topic of the presentation?*

3. Include Accurate Information

You should be able to answer the following questions:

- *Is the information to be presented relevant and accurate?*
- *Have all sources been cited as references?*

4. Plan the Slide Show

You should be able to answer the following question:

- *Did I create an outline of the presentation before starting any design work on the computer?*

Slide Show Design and Layout Guidelines:

When creating a slide show presentation, consider the following guidelines:

1. Consistency

- The design and layout of your slide show should be consistent with other documents used in your business.

2. Background Colors

- Use a background color that does not distract the attention of the audience.
- Keep the background consistent throughout the slide show.

3. Color Scheme

- Use colors that are consistent with those already established for your business.

4. Typefaces (Fonts)

- Use no more than two to three typefaces (fonts) throughout your slide show.
- Use a font that is easy to read and a font size that can easily be seen from the furthest corner of the room.
- Use font colors that make text easy to read when placed on a background.

5. Text

- Keep lines of text brief on each slide.
- Limit the information to include key points only.
- Limit lines of text to five or six lines per slide.
- Highlight key words with bold, italic, or underline effects, but use these effects sparingly.
- Introduce each line of text individually to focus audience attention.

6. Transitions

- Keep the transition effect from slide to slide the same so as to not distract or "cheapen" the look of your slide show.

7. Sound Effects

- Limit the use of sound effects to minimize distraction.

8. Animation

- Limit the use of animation to minimize distraction.

9. Graphic Images

- Use graphic images to help illustrate key points in your slide show.
- Choose graphics that are consistent in style, design, color, and size.

Now let's learn how Shaun Decker created a Promotional Slide Show for his business plan

Shaun Decker's Promotional Slide Show

Shaun decided to create a short slide show presentation to inform and promote Decker's Digital Desktop. His audience is expected to be adult business professionals in the Pleasant Landing community. Shaun will store the presentation on a laptop computer to show to his customers onsite at their locations. Using his brochure and advertisement as a guide, Shaun created the following outline for his slide show presentation:

Slide Show Presentation Outline

Slide #1: Introduction
Title:	Introducing Decker's Digital Desktop The image of your future
Text:	Shaun Decker, Owner, 123 Prescott Ave, Pleasant Landing, NY 19999 Phone: 315-999-9797, www.DeckersDigitalDesktop.com

Slide #2: About the Company
Title:	Who is Decker's Digital Desktop?
Text:	Decker's Digital Desktop was founded in 2006 for the purpose of providing Pleasant Landing area businesses with a one-stop source for all their printing needs. Using state-of-the-art technology, the company produces professional quality print and electronic documents.

Slide #3: Products and Services Provided
Title:	Products and Services Provided by Decker's Digital Desktop
Text 1:	*Print Documents Available:* Business Cards, Letterhead, Brochures
Text 2:	*Word Processing Services:* Reports, Resumes, Books, Catalogs, And More!
Text 3:	*Electronic Documents:* Web Site Development, Presentation Development

Slide #4: Introductory Offer
Title:	Introductory Offer: Get Free Business Cards!
Text:	Get 100 Free Business Cards with your first purchase of 500 cards or more

Slide #5: Closing
Title:	Thank you for Considering Decker's Digital Desktop: The Image of Your Future
Text:	Visit us online for special offers and product updates at www.DeckersDigitalDesktop.com

With his slide show presentation outline complete, Shaun was now ready to create his promotional slide show using Microsoft PowerPoint. To create a consistent business identity and image, Shaun used his brochure and newspaper advertisement as guides.

Shaun decided that he would print out each slide from the slide show on one sheet of paper and include it as a supplemental attachment in his business plan.

Shaun Decker's completed "Promotional Slide Show" is provided on the next page.

Shaun Decker's Promotional Slide Show:

Slide 1

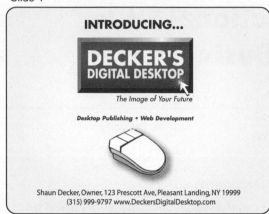

Slide 2

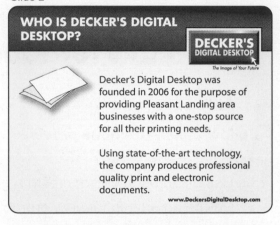

Slide 3

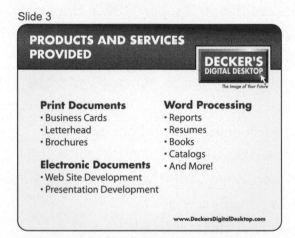

Slide 4

Slide 5

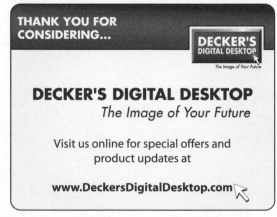

Now it's your turn to create a Promotional Slide Show for your business plan

Project 17:
Create a Promotional Slide Show for Your Business Plan

Follow the instructions provided below.

1. Using Microsoft Word, create a new document.
2. Create an outline for your promotional slide show presentation for your business. Use the "Overview" notes and Shaun Decker's "Slide Show Presentation Outline" as a guide. ***Note:*** *You are required to include a minimum of* <u>*five*</u> *slides in your presentation.*
3. Save the outline as "Project17_Outline" to the "My Business Plan" folder.
4. Print a copy of your outline.
5. Open the file "Project17_Slide_Show_Planning_Form" from the "Teen Entrepreneur" folder installed from the Data CD. Print a copy of the document and follow the instructions provided. ***Note:*** *You will need Adobe Acrobat Reader to view and print this document.*
6. Using Microsoft PowerPoint, create a new presentation.
7. Using your outline and the "Slide Show Presentation Planning Form" as a guide, create your Promotional Slide Show Presentation for your business. Remember, you are required to include a minimum of <u>five</u> slides in your presentation.
8. Carefully proofread each slide for accuracy and format.
9. Save the file as "Project17_Slide_Show" to the "My Business Plan" folder.
10. Print a copy of your slide show. Specify the print range to include all slides so that they all fit on one page.

    Keep the document in a secure place as you will need to add it to your Business Plan at the conclusion of this simulation.

Courtesy of Junior Achievement.

Ilana Rothbein of Manasquan, NJ
Company: Chores-For-Charity

It's not all about making a buck; it's about giving one too. 17-year-old Ilana Rothbein and her incredibly innovative organization, Chores-For-Charity, personify what it truly means to give.

Ilana had always wanted to organize a fundraiser, but found it extremely difficult while juggling schoolwork, sports, social activities, and work. So Ilana decided to donate the money from her babysitting jobs to f.a.c.e.s., NYU hospital's charitable organization which helps improve the lives of people with epilepsy. In one year, she donated almost 50 hours of her time babysitting and nearly $500 to f.a.c.e.s. Ilana thought, "if those hours could be considered community service, then I could get a lot of kids involved in this type of charitable work."

Ilana soon turned that thought into a reality. The premise behind the Chores-For-Charity program is that students may earn community service credit from their school or house of worship by donating a portion of their earnings (from part-time jobs, summer jobs, or odd jobs) to a charitable organization. The hours that the students worked to donate their earnings would qualify for community service.

Since its launch in December 2003, Chores-For-Charity has received support from many individuals, schools, and companies, and most importantly, continues to provide even more reason for students to give.

For more information on Chores-For-Charity and to find out how you can become involved, visit Ilana's Web site at: *www.choresforcharity.com*.

Project 18: Creating the Executive Summary

Section of Your Business Plan

Approximate Completion Time: 1 hour

INCLUDED IN THIS SECTION:

- Overview of the Executive Summary
- See It In Action with Shaun Decker
- Now It's Your Turn to Build Your Business Plan

SOFTWARE REQUIRED:

- Microsoft Word

Business Plan Checklist

✓ Project 1:   Choosing Your Teen-based Business
✓ Project 2:   Company Description
✓ Project 3:   Logo and Tagline
✓ Project 4:   Description of Products and Services
✓ Project 5:   Market Analysis
✓ Project 6:   Business Card
✓ Project 7:   Company Letterhead
✓ Project 8:   Marketing Plan
✓ Project 9:   Operating Plan
✓ Project 10: Schedule of Startup Funds Required
✓ Project 11: Customer Prospect Database
✓ Project 12: Introductory Promotional Letter
✓ Project 13: Three-Panel Brochure
✓ Project 14: Newspaper Advertisement
✓ Project 15: Owner's Resume
✓ Project 16: Projected Income Statement
✓ Project 17: Promotional Slide Show
  Project 18: Executive Summary
  Project 19: Business Plan Cover Page
  Project 20: Final Assembly of Your Business Plan
  Project 21: Company Web Site Homepage (*optional*)

The Executive Summary

THE TEEN ENTREPRENEUR

YOUR OBJECTIVE:

To produce the following section of your business plan:
• the Executive Summary

BACKGROUND INFORMATION BEFORE YOU BEGIN:

What is the Executive Summary section of a Business Plan?

While appearing first, the Executive Summary section of a business plan is written last. The **Executive Summary** is a miniature version of the business plan and usually contains a key point or two from most sections of the plan. It is a brief statement or account that covers the substance and main points of your company. The Executive Summary should be no longer than one to two pages and should give the reader of your business plan a quick "snapshot" of your business and the direction in which it is heading.

What's Included in the Executive Summary?

The Executive Summary of a business plan usually includes the following components:

1. **Introduction**
   The introduction should include a short summary of the business, the form of ownership, and one or two key characteristics of the business. The introduction should be written in such a way that it entices readers to want to read the business plan.

2. **Summary of Products and Services**
   The summary of products and services should include a brief overview of the products and/or services offered by the business.

3. **Market Summary**
   The market summary should include a brief overview of the target market and key components of the market analysis section of the business plan.

4. **Competitive Position**

   The competitive position section should include a statement of how the business will position itself against its competitors.

5. **Financial Position**

   The financial position section should summarize key financial points from the business plan. This section usually includes a summary of the funds required to start the business and a summary of projected income.

6. **Mission Statement**

   A mission statement should describe the goals and objectives of the business.

7. **Vision Statement**

   The vision statement should be a statement about where the business will find itself in the future.

Now let's look at Shaun Decker's Executive Summary section of his business plan

Shaun Decker's
Executive Summary

Shaun was nearing the completion of his business plan and was excited to write the Executive Summary section. Using the information from previously completed sections, Shaun began writing the "Executive Summary" for his business plan.

> Shaun Decker's completed "Executive Summary" section of his plan is provided on the next two pages.

Shaun Decker's Executive Summary:

Executive Summary

I. Introduction

Decker's Digital Desktop was founded in 2006 for the purpose of providing area businesses with a one-stop source for quality desktop publishing products and services. The business is operated from the home of Shaun Decker, Proprietor, who is the sole employee of the business.

The company can be characterized as a startup business with considerable growth opportunities.

More information about the company can be found in various parts of this business plan.

II. Products and Services

Decker's Digital Desktop specializes in providing a variety of high quality print and electronic documents including:
- Business Cards
- Letterhead
- Brochures
- Web Site Development
- Presentation Development
- Word Processing Services

More information can be found in the "Description of Products and Services" and "Marketing Plan" sections of this business plan.

III. Market Summary

The target market of Decker's Digital Desktop is adult professionals who work or own small businesses in the Pleasant Landing community. Eighty percent of all businesses in the Pleasant Landing community are considered small businesses. Since small businesses often do not have the funds available to employ desktop publishers, and given the fact that there are only a handful of competitors in the area, there is a need for Decker's Digital Desktop.

More information can be found in the "Market Analysis" section of this business plan.

IV. Competitive Position

There are four other desktop publishing businesses in the Pleasant Landing area. Of the four, only one offers Web site development as a service. This creates a niche for Decker's Digital Desktop since electronic document development will be offered. Since Decker's Digital Desktop will be operating as a home-based business, overhead expenses will be minimized. This provides Decker's Digital Desktop with a competitive advantage in offering lower prices than its competitors. At startup, Decker's Digital Desktop will also utilize several marketing techniques to attract new customers.

More information can be found in the "Market Analysis" and "Marketing Plan" sections of this plan.

1

Shaun Decker's Executive Summary continued:

V. Financial Position

The estimated funds required to start Decker's Digital Desktop are $3,337.78. To cover the startup funds, the owner will obtain a business loan in the amount of $5,000, which will be repaid using profits obtained from the business.

The projected first year's income is $8,297.67. This number is expected to grow steadily as Decker's Digital Desktop is committed to maintaining excellent customer service and add more products and services over time.

More information can be found in the "Schedule of Startup Funds Required" and the "Projected Income Statement" sections of this business plan.

VI. Mission Statement

The mission of Decker's Digital Desktop is to provide small businesses with the highest quality print and electronic documents at lower than competitive prices while earning a reputation of excellent customer service.

To achieve our mission, Decker's Digital Desktop commits to the following:

1. Follow the philosophy that our customers are and will always remain our first priority
2. Use only the highest quality materials in our products
3. Minimize overhead expenses and pass these savings on to the customer.
4. Never be satisfied with the status quo

VII. Vision Statement

By 2010, Decker's Digital Desktop will be a highly visible company known as the leader in the regional desktop publishing industry. The company is noted for the highest standards in quality and customer service.

2

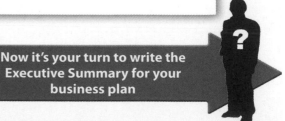
Now it's your turn to write the Executive Summary for your business plan

Project 18:
Create the Executive Summary
Section of Your Business Plan

Follow the instructions provided below.

1. Using Microsoft Word, retrieve the file "Project18_Worksheet" from the "Teen Entrepreneur" folder installed from the Data CD.

2. Type your name and the current date in the header section of page 1 in the document.

3. Follow the instructions provided in the document to complete the worksheet.

4. Carefully proofread your work for accuracy and format.

5. Print a copy of the completed worksheet.

6. Save the completed worksheet to the "My Business Plan" folder.

7. Using Microsoft Word, open the file "Project18_Template" from the "Teen Entrepreneur" folder installed from the Data CD.

8. Complete all of the sections provided in the "Project18_Template" file to write the "Executive Summary" section of your business plan. Use the "Overview" notes and Shaun Decker's "Executive Summary" as a guide.
   Tip: Copy and paste some or all of the information you included in the worksheet.

9. Carefully proofread your work for accuracy and format.

10. Save the file as "Project18_Exec_Summary" to the "My Business Plan" folder.

11. Print a copy of the document.

Project 19: Creating the Cover Page

For Your Business Plan

Approximate Completion Time: .5 hours

INCLUDED IN THIS SECTION:

- Overview of the Business Plan Cover Page
- See It In Action with Shaun Decker
- Now It's Your Turn to Build Your Business Plan

SOFTWARE REQUIRED:

- Microsoft Word

Business Plan Checklist

✓ Project 1:   Choosing Your Teen-based Business
✓ Project 2:   Company Description
✓ Project 3:   Logo and Tagline
✓ Project 4:   Description of Products and Services
✓ Project 5:   Market Analysis
✓ Project 6:   Business Card
✓ Project 7:   Company Letterhead
✓ Project 8:   Marketing Plan
✓ Project 9:   Operating Plan
✓ Project 10: Schedule of Startup Funds Required
✓ Project 11: Customer Prospect Database
✓ Project 12: Introductory Promotional Letter
✓ Project 13: Three-Panel Brochure
✓ Project 14: Newspaper Advertisement
✓ Project 15: Owner's Resume
✓ Project 16: Projected Income Statement
✓ Project 17: Promotional Slide Show
✓ Project 18: Executive Summary
   Project 19: Business Plan Cover Page
   Project 20: Final Assembly of Your Business Plan
   Project 21: Company Web Site Homepage (*optional*)

The Business Plan Cover Page

THE TEEN ENTREPRENEUR

YOUR OBJECTIVE:

To produce the following section of your business plan:
- the Business Plan Cover Page

BACKGROUND INFORMATION BEFORE YOU BEGIN:

The Importance of the Business Plan Cover Page

In business, image is everything! People do judge a book by its cover. And, people will judge a business by its business plan's cover. With that said, the importance of creating a professional, attractive cover page for your business plan cannot be stressed enough. After all, the cover page is the first impression a business will make on prospective readers. You never get a second chance to make a good first impression!

As you have learned from this book, it takes a great deal of time to create a business plan. Shortly, you will be turning in your business plan to your instructor to be graded. The cover page will be the first thing your instructor will evaluate. Your cover page design should reflect the time and effort you have spent developing your business plan.

What's Included on the Business Plan Cover Page?

The cover page of the business plan should include the following information:

1. The company name and/or logo
2. The title "Business Plan"
3. The month and year the business plan was created
4. The name and title of the person preparing the document
5. A sentence that reads: "This document contains confidential and proprietary information belonging exclusively to <company name>."
6. The address and telephone number of the business

Now let's look at Shaun Decker's Business Plan Cover Page

Shaun Decker's
Business Plan Cover Page

Shaun Decker had just one simple step left to complete his business plan: to create the cover page using Microsoft Word.

> Shaun Decker's completed "Cover Page" is provided below.

**Decker's Digital Desktop
Business Plan**

September 2006

Prepared by Shaun Decker, Owner

123 Prescott Avenue
Pleasant Landing, NY 19999
(315) 999-9797

This document contains confidential and proprietary information belonging
exclusively to Decker's Digital Desktop

**Now it's your turn to create a Cover
Page for your business plan**

Project 19:
Create the Cover Page for Your Business Plan

Follow the instructions provided below.

1. Using Microsoft Word, create a new document.
2. Create the cover page for your business plan. Use the "Overview" notes and Shaun Decker's "Cover Page" as a guide.
   Your cover page should include the following:
   a. The company name and/or logo
   b. The title "Business Plan"
   c. The month and year the business plan was created
   d. The name and title of the person preparing the document
   e. A sentence that reads:
   "This document contains confidential and proprietary information belonging exclusively to <company name>."
   f. The address and telephone number of the business
3. Save the completed file as "Project19_Cover" to the "My Business Plan" folder.
4. Carefully proofread your work for accuracy and format.
5. Print a copy of the document.

Project 20:
Final Assembly of
Your Business Plan

Approximate Completion Time: 1 hour

Business Plan Checklist

✓ Project 1:   Choosing Your Teen-based Business
✓ Project 2:   Company Description
✓ Project 3:   Logo and Tagline
✓ Project 4:   Description of Products and Services
✓ Project 5:   Market Analysis
✓ Project 6:   Business Card
✓ Project 7:   Company Letterhead
✓ Project 8:   Marketing Plan
✓ Project 9:   Operating Plan
✓ Project 10:   Schedule of Startup Funds Required
✓ Project 11:   Customer Prospect Database
✓ Project 12:   Introductory Promotional Letter
✓ Project 13:   Three-Panel Brochure
✓ Project 14:   Newspaper Advertisement
✓ Project 15:   Owner's Resume
✓ Project 16:   Projected Income Statement
✓ Project 17:   Promotional Slide Show
✓ Project 18:   Executive Summary
✓ Project 19:   Business Plan Cover Page
   Project 20:   Final Assembly of Your Business Plan
   Project 21:   Company Web Site Homepage (*optional*)

INCLUDED IN THIS SECTION:

- Overview of the Final Assembly of Your Business Plan
- See It In Action with Shaun Decker
- Now It's Your Turn to Build Your Business Plan

SOFTWARE REQUIRED:

   • None

Final Assembly of Your Business Plan

THE TEEN ENTREPRENEUR

YOUR OBJECTIVE:

- To assemble all of the sections and attachments of your business plan

BACKGROUND INFORMATION BEFORE YOU BEGIN:

The Importance of Assembling a Business Plan Properly

While the format and the order of sections vary from one business plan to another, careful consideration should be given to its final format and assembly.

All good business plans share three things in common:

1. **A Professional Format**
   - Text should be clear and easy to read.
   - Each section should contain bold headings.
   - Fonts that are unprofessional and difficult to read should be avoided.

2. **Logically Ordered**
   - The individual sections of a business plan should be organized in a logical order.
   - The business plan should create a step-by-step walk-through of your business.
   - After reading the business plan, the reader should have a clear idea of the visions and goals that will help make the business a success.

3. **Well-Written**
   - The business plan should be written using short, concise sentences.
   - The business plan should be mistake-free.

The Order of the Business Plan

Using the projects you have previously completed in this book, you now have all the components to complete your business plan and become a real teen entrepreneur.

When complete, your business plan will be organized in the following order:

1. Cover Page
2. Executive Summary
3. Company Description
4. Description of Products and Services
5. Market Analysis
6. Marketing Plan
7. Operating Plan
8. Schedule of Startup Funds Required
9. Projected Income Statement
10. Owner's Resume
11. Supplemental Attachments:
    - Logo and Tagline
    - Business Card
    - Company Letterhead
    - Customer Prospect Database
    - Introductory Promotional Letter
    - Brochure
    - Newspaper Advertisement
    - Promotional Slide Show Presentation
    - Web Site Homepage (*Optional: complete Project 21*)

Before you begin the final assembly of your business plan, let's take a look at Shaun Decker's finished business plan.

Now let's look at Shaun Decker's completed Business Plan

Shaun Decker's Completed Business Plan

Shaun Awaits His Parents' Decision

Shaun did it! He successfully completed all of the components of his business plan for Decker's Digital Desktop. Shaun's next step was to assemble all of the sections of his business plan and then present it to his parents.

Shaun was confident that, after reading his business plan, his parents would see the hard work, research, and effort that went into preparing it. He was hopeful that they would conclude that Decker's Digital Desktop was a good investment and loan him the required startup money.

Shaun knew the importance of presenting a professionally written, well-formatted business plan. Before assembling his final business plan, Shaun carefully reviewed, evaluated, and edited each section and then made several formatting and structural revisions.

Before handing the business plan over to his parents, Shaun decided to complete one more project that he would add as a supplemental attachment: a company Web site (see Project 21).

At this point, there was nothing more that Shaun Decker could do but anxiously await the decision of his parents...

To view Shaun Decker's completed "Business Plan," open the file "Deckers_Business_Plan" from the "Teen Entrepreneur" folder installed from the Data CD.

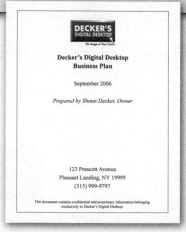

The Final Decision...

Shaun's parents, Jeff and Caroline Decker, were nothing less than impressed by Shaun's business plan. They each agreed that Shaun's business plan was well done. It was a professional, well-written document that demonstrated Decker's Digital Desktop could be a success. They agreed to lend Shaun the $5,000 required to start Decker's Digital Desktop.

Shaun was elated! He couldn't wait to get the ball rolling with his new business venture. He was ready to tackle the challenges that lie ahead with owning his own business. Shaun was truly on his way to becoming a successful teen entrepreneur.

Now it's your turn to assemble your Business Plan

Project 20:
Assemble Your Business Plan

Follow the instructions provided below.

1. Using Microsoft Word, create a new document. Save the document as "Business Plan Complete" to the "My Business Plan" folder.

2. Insert the following footer to appear on every page in the document, excluding page 1 (which will be your cover page):

    \<Your business name\>: Business Plan   Page #

3. Retrieve each file shown in the table below from the "My Business Plan" folder.

4. Copy and paste the text from each Word document and the cells (containing data) from each Excel workbook into the "Business Plan Complete" document in the order shown in the table below. Separate each section using a page break. Use Shaun Decker's completed "Business Plan" as a guide.

Order	Section	File Name
1.	Cover Page	Project19_Cover
2.	Executive Summary	Project18_Exec_Summary
3.	Company Description	Project2_Company_Description
4.	Description of Products and Services	Project4_Products_Services
5.	Market Analysis	Project5_Market_Analysis
6.	Marketing Plan	Project8_Marketing_Plan
7.	Operating Plan	Project9_Operating_Plan
8.	Schedule of Startup Funds Required	Project10_Startup_Funds
9.	Projected Income Statement	Project16_Income_Statement
10.	Owner's Resume	Project15_Resume

5. Create a new page after the last page of the "Business Plan Complete" document.

(Continued on next page)

Project 20 Instructions Continued:

6. Create a "Supplemental Attachments" cover page by adding the following text to the new page you created in Step 5:

> Supplemental Attachments:
> Attachment A: Logo and Tagline
> Attachment B: Business Card
> Attachment C: Company Letterhead
> Attachment D: Customer Prospect Database
> Attachment E: Introductory Promotional Letter
> Attachment F: Brochure
> Attachment G: Newspaper Advertisement
> Attachment H: Promotional Slide Show Presentation
> Attachment I: Web Site Homepage (*add only if you completed Project 21*)

7. Proofread each section of your business plan very carefully. Make any necessary grammatical and/or formatting changes. Be sure that each section of the business plan is formatted consistently.

8. Print a copy of the "Business Plan Complete" document.

9. Retrieve a printed copy of each supplemental attachment document shown in Step 6 above. Place each document (in the order shown in Step 6 above) after the last page of your business plan (the "Supplemental Attachments" cover page).

10. Place the contents of your completed business plan in a three-ring view binder (*optional*).

11. Submit your finished business plan to your instructor.

Congratulations on Completing The Teen Entrepreneur!

By completing the projects in this book, you have taken the first step to becoming a successful teen entrepreneur. You now have the necessary background and information to start your own real teen-based business. It is our hope that you use your business plan and the marketing materials you produced to start your own real business. If you do so, we'd love to hear about it. You can e-mail your teen entrepreneur story to us at: TTE@bepublishing.com.

Project 21:
Creating a Web Site Homepage

For Your Business Plan (*Optional*)

Approximate Completion Time: 1-2 hours

W W W

INCLUDED IN THIS SECTION:

- Overview of the Homepage of a Web Site
- See It In Action with Shaun Decker
- Now It's Your Turn to Build Your Business Plan

SOFTWARE REQUIRED:

- Microsoft FrontPage or Any Web Site Design Software

Business Plan Checklist

- ✓ Project 1: Choosing Your Teen-based Business
- ✓ Project 2: Company Description
- ✓ Project 3: Logo and Tagline
- ✓ Project 4: Description of Products and Services
- ✓ Project 5: Market Analysis
- ✓ Project 6: Business Card
- ✓ Project 7: Company Letterhead
- ✓ Project 8: Marketing Plan
- ✓ Project 9: Operating Plan
- ✓ Project 10: Schedule of Startup Funds Required
- ✓ Project 11: Customer Prospect Database
- ✓ Project 12: Introductory Promotional Letter
- ✓ Project 13: Three-Panel Brochure
- ✓ Project 14: Newspaper Advertisement
- ✓ Project 15: Owner's Resume
- ✓ Project 16: Projected Income Statement
- ✓ Project 17: Promotional Slide Show
- ✓ Project 18: Executive Summary
- ✓ Project 19: Business Plan Cover Page
- ✓ Project 20: Business Plan Assembled
-   Project 21: Company Web Site Homepage (*optional*)

The Homepage of a Web Site

THE TEEN ENTREPRENEUR

YOUR OBJECTIVE:

To produce the following item to be included in your business plan:
- the Homepage of your company's Web site

BACKGROUND INFORMATION BEFORE YOU BEGIN:

The Importance of the Homepage

Just about every business in existence today advertises and promotes by using a Web site. While a Web site can range from a few to hundreds of pages, the **homepage** is without question, the most important page of a Web site.

The homepage is the one page that will be seen by every Web site visitor. It can either keep visitors interested or turn them away.

Homepage Design Tips and Guidelines:

When designing the homepage for your business, consider the following design tips and guidelines:

- The homepage should provide a friendly, welcoming layout and design.
- Limit the typefaces (fonts) in your homepage. Use a font that is standard on most computers, such as arial, times new roman, or verdana.
- Do not overload the homepage with too much information.
- Use a color and scheme that is consistent with your logo.
- Use graphic images that relate to your type of business.
- Before starting on the computer, plan the content, layout, and design of the homepage on paper.

Now let's look at Shaun Decker's Homepage

Shaun Decker's Homepage

Knowing that he would need a Web presence to advertise and promote his business, Shaun decided to create the homepage of a Web site for Decker's Digital Desktop. Shaun would use the homepage as a basis to create the remaining pages of the Web site at a later date. He would include a screenshot of the homepage as a supplemental attachment in his business plan.

After sketching several design possibilities and using the content from his brochure and slide show as a guide, Shaun created a homepage that looked professional and captured the essence of his business.

> The homepage of Shaun Decker's Web site is provided below.

Shaun Decker's homepage of his Web site:

Project 21:
Create the Homepage of Your Company's Web Site for Your Business Plan

Follow the instructions provided below.

1. Open the file "Project21_Homepage_Planning_Form" from the "Teen Entrepreneur" folder installed from the Data CD. Print a copy of the document and follow the instructions provided. ***Note:*** *You will need Adobe Acrobat Reader to view and print this document.*

2. Using Microsoft FrontPage, create a new one page Web site. Name the Web site "Project21_Homepage" and store it in the "My Business Plan" folder.

3. Use the information you added to the "Homepage Planning Form" to create the homepage for your company's Web site. Use the "Overview" notes and Shaun Decker's "Homepage" as a guide.

4. Carefully proofread your work for accuracy and format.

5. Print a copy of the homepage and add it to your business plan according to the instructions provided in Project 20.